ALL THE KING'S

PREPARING TO REIGN

PART 1

Bishop William A. Lee, Jr.

ISBN 979-8890744975

Table of Contents

FOREWORD

Search the pages of the Old Testament and you will discover that large portions of this ancient book of history, law, prophecy, and wisdom are dedicated to telling the story and preserving the writings of one particular figure, a remarkable man named David. Of all the characters whose stories are recounted in the Jewish Scriptures, David is probably better known to us than any other.

This is a felicitous situation, because the chronicle of David's life is a textbook of spiritual instruction for those who are willing to read and learn. Tracing his story from shepherd boy to king of his nation permits Christians to learn lessons of humility, faith, trust, confidence, integrity, spiritual power, personal failure, and heartfelt repentance. .

The stories about David become more complex and elaborate when we study not only the king, but all the king's men. The actions of his family, friends, and foes reveal to us how our own lives can be shaped and affected by our companions—for good or ill.

All the King's Men is a marvelous book crafted from a series of sermons preached by William A. Lee Jr. to real-life people living authentic workaday lives. He is loved by his congregation, and he is one of my favorite preachers. Bill and I have been friends for a long time. Back in college days, we spent hours in classes together and lived on the same hall in the dormitory. I came to admire his grasp of Scripture as a student, and over the years I have come to appreciate even more deeply his proficiency in speaking for God. He is a highly respected preacher of the Word in the pulpits of the largest churches in our denomination. As a pastor, he has led significant congregations in meaningful ministry.

I commend this noteworthy book to your reading and study. If you are a preacher, you will find inspiration and resources to undergird your own sermons. If you are simply a man or woman who loves the Word of God and desires to learn and live it, you will discover rich reserves of practical truth.

One of the chief truths taught by Bill Lee as he examines King David and his peers (and hopefully taken to heart by all of us who read this remarkable book) is the power of influence—others upon us; ours upon others. Donald Phillips, writing in Lincoln on Leadership, advises, "It is the leader's role to lift followers out of their everyday selves up to a higher level of awareness, motivation, and commitment."

Be moved by what you read to touch and make a difference in someone's life.

Dr. Mark L. Williams

General Overseer

Church of God

DEDICATION

It is with profound feelings of gratitude and love that I dedicate these writings to the woman, who after God, that I owe my very existence-My Amazing Mother, **the late Essie C. Lee.**

As a single mother of seven her selfless dedication and sacrifice produced a family who continues to carry her legacy long after her departure in 2006. Her wisdom, wit, and ability to continue to believe God in spite of seemingly insurmountable odds continues to speak to me and encourage me daily. I am thankful to God who gifted us with this angel for so many years. I truly miss her and I am eternally grateful.

To my lovely wife, lifelong partner Sheila Renee Lee for her steadfast love, patience, and companionship. Thank you for believing in me.

Special Thanks

To all who have contributed their effort, advice and typing. Dr Sharon Apopa, Elder Esther Trott and Lois Burgess of Bermuda. My Sister Rachelle Lee of Springfield, Massachusetts; Angelia Keinlen of Cleveland, Tennessee.

My first Pastor Dr. Ronald E. Peters, the late Dr. Joseph E. Jackson and the late Dr. Luther Painter for seeing a writer in me even before I did.

My Brothers and Sisters: Trecitia Campbell, Barry Campbell, Melvin and Jacquelyn Washington, Rachelle Lee, Marcella Lee, Dr. Patricia Lee, Jamahl and Anisha Campbell, Lewis Lee, Erin Washington, and Miles Lee.

To Heritage Worship Center in Hamilton Bermuda where I served during the time in which this book was birthed. Daytona Deliverance Church of God in Daytona Beach, Florida, and the wonderful staff of Leeds Press.

PREFACE

In this book, we will discover how the many relationships that David made during his life's journey impacted him both negatively and positively as he endeavored to walk into his purpose in life. We need to understand that God desires to take us all to a place of destiny. He wants us to reign in the area in which He has anointed us and in which He has called us to excel. Along the course of that journey, going from here to there, He will allow people to come into our lives as well as remove others from our lives, to work out His purpose in us. Some of these people are good people who will bless us, but then some of these people are not so good and will cause us pain.

When we understand that our God is on the throne and that He reigns and super-reigns, rules, and super-rules, we come to the understanding that even those people who come into our lives to cause us pain God can use for our good in order to take us to the place where He will have us reign.

Some of us get wounded, become upset, and allow those kinds of people to cripple us in our walk because we do not realize that God can even use and turn the activities of the devil to be a blessing for us. We see that acted out in the life of David, who grew to be Israel's greatest king.

"All the King's Men" is not gender related because we are going to find that there were also some women who played important parts in David's life.

"All the King's Men: *Book One – Preparing to Reign*" traces David's life from the Sheepfolds of Israel to his defeat of the giant Goliath and his covenant friendship with Jonathan, King Saul's son. We will meet

David's father, Jesse, who not only overlooks his youngest son, but rejects him as even worthy to participate in the special anointing ceremony Samuel was sent to Bethlehem to perform. We, of course, meet the Prophet of God, Samuel who not only anoints young David, but also imparts his spirit of integrity into this young shepherd boy. We will meet David's brothers, especially his oldest brother and the first born of Jesse's eight sons, who also belittles and rebukes David as he tries to accomplish what God has called him to do. We will watch as David defeats the mighty Goliath, serves in King Saul's court, and enjoys a special relationship with his son, Jonathan.

You will want to continue your study of "All the King's Men" in *Book Two – Establishing a New Kingdom* where David is literally run out of the palace and runs for his life, pursued by King Saul and his army. David goes from the palace to the wilderness, and on to the cave of Adullam to complete his training for reigning under the guiding hand of Almighty God Himself. God uses many relationships during this journey to prepare this shepherd boy to reign as Israel's greatest king!

SECTION ONE

David Preparing to Reign

Preparation is the pre-departure time when one counts the cost of the journey and sets aside the resources that will take them to where they want to go. Preparation is the pre-battle time when one sharpens their weapon and strengthens their shield to take them through to victory.

And Samuel said to Saul, thou hast done foolishly: Thou hast not kept the commandment of the Lord thy God, which he commanded thee: for now, would the Lord have established thy kingdom upon Israel forever. But now thy kingdom shall not continue: the Lord hath sought him a man after his own heart, and the Lord hath commanded him to be captain over his people, because thou hast not kept that which the Lord commanded thee. (1 Samuel 13:13-14)

I must confess to you that I am thankful to God that some of the prayers that I have prayed were not answered. I say this with the advantage of hindsight and with the realization that there are some things that I asked for that I simply was not prepared and mature enough to handle. I did not have what I needed on the inside of me to handle those things properly at that time and place in my life. In other words, I wanted to reign in certain places with certain things that my level of preparation was not where I needed it to be for those things to be a blessing to me as opposed to becoming a curse.

Regardless of what arena in life one finds oneself, we all have to agree that there is nothing more beneficial than preparation.

Preparation

There is nothing more beneficial than preparation.

Preparation - is what causes one to count the cost of their journey and lay aside the resources that will hopefully take them where they want to go. Preparation is what makes a person sharpen their sword and shine their shield long before the battle ever begins. The prepared person is one who understands that practice is just as important as the game. If you want something done right and done with excellence, there is no better person to call upon than the person who is **prepared.**

On the other hand, there are very few things that are as painful and frustrating as having to deal with someone who has not taken the time to **prepare.** For example, having to sit through a presentation on the job when it is painfully obvious the presenter has not taken time to research the topic of discussion, and does not know whether they are coming or going. Equally frustrating is having to deal with someone who thinks that because they have been on the job for a while, they do not have to take the time to **prepare** anymore.

Ever have to listen to a musical presentation that is thrown together because certain singers or musicians do not feel the need to show up for rehearsal? Ever suffer through a sermon in which the preacher has not taken the time to pray and study? He ends up talking about himself and anything else that pops into his head instead of it being all about God.

I dare say that some people were unprepared for marriage when they got married. When they walked down the aisle they were prepared to have a wedding, but not prepared to have a marriage. Now everyone in that household is miserable. There are some people who were ready to have sex but were not prepared to be parents. Now they don't want to take care of the results of their behavior.

There are people in positions in church who got there based on all the wrong criteria. When we look at the lack of fruit from their labor, it is painfully obvious that they were not prepared to step into that position. Indeed, it is a painful thing to see someone attempting to function within a place or an activity in which there has not been proper preparation. Are you prepared for what God is calling you to do?

Today's preparation determines tomorrow's achievement.

One of the things that has been stifling the church for decades is this false mentality that God frowns upon preparation. As a Bible student and a seminarian, I had to sit through sermons preached by insecure men telling me that education is not necessary. They told us all we had to do was stand in the pulpit, just open our mouths, and the Lord would give us what to say. I would have to sit there while they used rhymes saying we don't need theology, we need knee-ology, and calling the seminary a cemetery. They frowned upon preparation under the guise that the Holy Spirit will help us to do everything. However, I have learned that when God is looking for someone that He can consistently use for His glory and His honor; He is looking for someone who has been prepared for that position.

The fact of the matter is that many of us are too lazy to pursue the things that God has for us. If we are really going to be used by Him, we have to be prepared. To ascend to one's throne of destiny and to reign in the place of God's assignment is not an easy task. It is a journey that is filled with obstacles and even surprises that preparation will help us overcome and one that requires **preparation through process.** God will not promote us or allow us to ascend to our place of destiny without the assurance that we are prepared to handle the blessings that He has for us. We won't be bumped up a grade. We won't be able to skip class. We won't be excused from learning. We must be faithful to serve where we are called with the right attitude of the heart before we can be promoted to that next level.

CHAPTER 1

David Was Faithful

And he sent, and brought him in. Now he was ruddy, and withal of a beautiful countenance, and goodly to look to. And the LORD said, Arise, anoint him: for this is he. (1 Samuel 16:12)

David did not have anything behind his name. He did not have a very good résumé. Unlike Saul, David did not have any of the physical attributes of a king. The Bible says that Saul was head and shoulders above everybody around him. He looked like a king. He walked like a king. Saul was not just tall; he had what they call, "presence." Did you ever meet somebody with "presence"? As soon as they walk in the room you just know that this is an important individual. Well, Saul had it all together on the outside. He was stately. He was handsome. He looked like a king.

The Bible had a very different description of the shepherd boy David. In 1 Samuel 16:12 it describes David as "ruddy and withal of a beautiful countenance and goodly to look to." David did not have all of the exterior things Saul did. Some Bible scholars believe that he was a red-haired child with a nice, cute face, but he was not at all like Saul, physically speaking.

Let's take a look at David's résumé. He did not hold any important positions. He did not have any great references to give when Samuel showed up at their house to anoint the next king. David was simply serving as a shepherd boy. This was the job that nobody wanted. Men in David's time dreamed of being craftsmen and warriors. They wanted to be anything but a shepherd. David was put in this position because he was the youngest of eight sons. The firstborn always received the great position, always were granted the blessings, and always got all of the good things. When David was born, he was the eighth of eight sons, so he was the one sent out into the field to do the job that nobody else wanted.

He did not have the looks, the prestige, or the outward appearance of a king yet God saw something in this young man that He could use for His glory. What God saw was a humble, submissive spirit that was brought about by doing what his earthly father told him to do, even though he thought it was unpleasant.

Faithful Shepherd

Therefore, my beloved brethren, be ye steadfast, unmovable, always abounding in the work of the Lord, forasmuch as you know that your labor is not in vain in the Lord. (1 Corinthians 15:58)

Every day he had to be faithful and watch the sheep in the rain, in the heat, in the snow, and when it was freezing cold. David was out there watching and protecting them from predators, finding lost sheep, and rescuing them from danger. He was out there shoveling sheep dung, shearing the sheep, feeding the sheep, and nursing the sick ones back to health. If you had interviewed David and asked, "How was your day?" he would just say, "Same sheep, different day." Every day David was out there just being faithful to the assignment that God had given him. Nobody was patting him on the back. Nobody was giving him certificates.

Nobody was acknowledging him. Nobody was talking about him when they greeted other family members. David was just in the background doing his job.

Anybody in ministry can be faithful over the glamorous jobs. Anybody can be faithful when everybody is watching you and everybody is applauding you. Anybody can be faithful when you are in the pulpit or leading praise and worship, and you have the attention of the masses. But the person who God wants to use to reign in a position of blessing is the kind of person who is going to be faithful in the background when nobody is looking. That's the kind of person who says, "I will be faithful whether they applaud me or whether they don't because I am in the service of my King. I am going to praise and give God glory whether they encourage or try to discourage me. That's alright with me because I am in the service of the King. If I have to walk this walk all by myself and have people criticizing me and questioning my sincerity, I'm going to be faithful."

God is looking for somebody who is going to be faithful in the labor and the position in which they presently find themselves in. God rewards faithfulness. God will open up a door that no man can shut. God will make a way where there does not seem to be a way. No one may reward you immediately, but God keeps a record and He is watching everything that you do. He will reward you if you are faithful so stay faithful. God honors faithfulness. He will reward you in due time.

However, it is always a mistake to promote somebody who is not faithful and effective where they are. How one handles small assignments is an indicator of how one will handle large assignments. One of my favorite characters in the Bible is Daniel. Daniel and the children of

Israel are off in captivity, in slavery, and being oppressed. They have been taken away from their homeland, yet the Bible says, "Daniel was preferred above the presidents and princes because an excellent spirit was in him" (Daniel 6:3). He had an excellent spirit. He had the spirit to excel. He had the spirit that says, "Whether they see me or whether they don't, whether things are going good or whether things are going bad, everything that I do I'm going to do for God to the best of my ability."

God wants the best that we have. When we're preaching, we need to give our best. If we are vacuuming the floor, we need to vacuum the floor so good that the angels in heaven are going to pause and watch us work for the Kingdom of God. God deserves our best. David was assigned a job that nobody else wanted but he did it with an excellent spirit. When anyone starts talking about a Shepherd, David's name will automatically come up because he gave God his best whether he was in the fields as a shepherd or in the palace as a king. He decided that if he was going to shovel sheep dung and watch over the sheep, he'd be the best at it. His goal was to go down in history as the greatest shepherd that ever lived. When we start talking about the attributes of God, we compare Him to a shepherd because of the actions of a man named David. David aspired to write it down on paper saying, "The Lord is my shepherd, I shall not want" (Psalm 23:1)

Character and Integrity Development

Whatever you do in word or deed do it all unto God and God will bless you. When you are laboring in obscurity it is just a part of the plan.

God had David assigned to this job to develop his **character and his integrity.** Whenever God has something great for a person it takes time to grow the roots and build the foundation. If you just build a little hut you don't have to have much of a foundation. You can just throw it up on the dirt. If you want to build a major building, however, the higher the building is going to go the deeper you have to dig.

Palm trees are able to stand up and withstand the winds of a hurricane. Did you ever see them when the winds are blowing, they are all bent over. They just wave back and forth and then after the storm is over, they just pop up and they are straight again. That happens because long before that palm tree broke the surface before it grew up it had to grow down. That's what we've got to understand as well. When God is about to do something and use us for something great, He first has to establish our roots. Things happen below the surface that are going to prepare us for what is ahead.

There has to be some growth that takes place when nobody is looking, behind closed doors, when you are lonely and weeping all by yourself. God wants you to grow tall so that when the winds of adversity blow, you will bend but you sure won't break.

When David was in this place all by himself God was preparing him to reign. As a matter of fact, it was out in the sheepfolds that God was preparing David by allowing him to practice his miracles. When he appeared before King Saul to take on Goliath, Saul said, "Hey, I looked at your resume and you haven't been a warrior. You haven't killed anybody. You haven't served in the Bermuda Regiment, the Mighty Marines or with Scotland Yards. You don't have any of these qualifications. Who do you think you are going before this giant?" David said, "You don't understand. While I may not have an impressive resume, I do have a testimony. Before I walked out before you and before anybody knew my name, I was practicing my miracles in the background. One day I was watching the sheep and a bear came into the sheepfold. The Spirit of the Lord came upon me, and I took out the bear. On another occasion a lion came into the sheepfold thinking that he was going to have a meal on my father's sheep. The Spirit of the God came upon me, and I took the lion by the beard, and I shook the life out of him. The same God that gave me the lion and the bear will surely give me this uncircumcised Philistine."

That's why when the giant came before him David said, "You're coming at me with a spear and a sword, but I come at you in the name of the Lord. I've been practicing my miracle. I've been faithful to God and now God has anointed me for such a time as this!"

Key Points:

To ascend to one's throne of destiny and to reign requires preparation through process.

God won't promote or allow us to reign until we're prepared to handle the blessings.

Benjamin Franklin said, "By failing to prepare you are preparing to fail."

Today's preparation determines tomorrow's achievement.

We won't be excused from learning the lessons.

We won't be allowed to bump up a grade.

We won't be able to skip class.

We must be faithful.

Grow down,

Then up!

Ask Yourself:

Am I giving God my best?

Am I being faithful where I am right now?

What does God see when He looks inside of me?

What has God been preparing me for?

Declare:

I might bend but I won't break. I will be faithful and endure for a night because I know joy comes in the morning. I am going down before I grow up because God is preparing me for my miracle. I've been prepared! I've been faithful and now God is about to use me.

CHAPTER 2

David's Heart Was Ready

**The LORD has sought for Himself a man after His own heart, and
the LORD has commanded him to be commander over His people.**
(1 Samuel 13:14 NKJV)

David's heart was ready. In the Bible the heart represents much
more than the instrument that pumps the blood throughout the body.
In the Scriptures the heart comprises our thoughts and is the seat of the
emotions. It is the innermost center of the natural conditions of man.
According to the Word of God, you are what's in your heart. Some people smile and try to act like they are alright, but they need to understand
that what's in their heart will eventually come out. They can try to fake
it; they can try to pretend but what is in the heart is going to come out.

You are what's in your heart!

It's All About the Heart

In Matthew 12:34 Jesus said, "Out of the abundance of the heart the
mouth speaketh." If you want to know what a person is all about, listen
to what they say because eventually what's in their heart is going to
come out. If they're bitter, angry, jealous, envious, and have hatred in
their heart toward you, sooner or later it will come out. If you want to
know what you're all about ask yourself, "What do I think about most of
the time?" Proverbs 23:7 says, "For as a man thinketh in his heart, so is

he." You are what's in your heart and sooner or later it's going to come out.

As in water face reflects face, so a man's heart reveals the man. (Proverbs 27:19 NKJV)

Some people stay in a relationship with people who exhibit destructive behavior. They make excuses for this behavior saying, "Oh, that's just the way they are but they really have a good heart, they just don't know how to bring it from their heart to their actions." The truth is people will judge you for your actions not by your intentions. What's in your heart is going to determine your actions. The thing about David that was so outstanding is that he had a heart after God. David did not possess position, prestige, power, money or even appearance but God saw something in his heart.

God sent Samuel to the anointing ceremony at Jesse's house. David's dad brought all of his brothers, all those men in the house that were robust, strong, tall, dark, and handsome before Samuel. The first one's name was Eliab and he came walking into the house and Samuel said, "Surely, this is the Lord's anointed." But God said, "Samuel, don't look upon his countenance, don't look upon the height of his stature because I have refused him."

The Lord seeth not as man seeth for man looketh on the outward appearance but God looks on the heart. (1 Samuel 16:7)

When God measures a man or a woman, he wraps a tape measurer around his or her heart and not around his/her head, biceps or chest. David was a man after God's own heart. What does it mean to be a "man after God's own heart?" It means "to have a heart in harmony with God." That means what is important to God becomes important to you.

What burdens God burdens you. When He speaks you listen and do what He says. You change what He wants you to change. You do what He wants you to do. You act like He wants you to act. You want as much of Him as you can possibly get. That's a person who has a heart after God. It doesn't matter what anybody says about you. It doesn't matter what anybody's expectations are of you. It doesn't matter how anybody wants you to act. You must seek to do what God tells you to do if you want to have a heart that is after God.

2 Chronicles 16:9 says, "*For the eye of the Lord runs to and fro throughout the whole earth to show himself strong in the behalf of them whose heart is perfect toward him.*" In other words, God is going throughout the earth looking for somebody who has a heart for Him. The problem is we are too impressed by our outward appearance. The person that has got the right clothes, the right hat, and drives the right car is the one that impresses us. We need to understand that God is not even looking at that. God is looking for someone who has a heart toward Him. Most of the problems that we have are due to the conditions of people's hearts. Disobedience is in the heart. Hatred is in the heart.

Broken-Hearted

God is not looking for a superstar. He is just looking for somebody who has a heart after Him. Part of the course David was on was to develop the condition of his heart. David was rejected by his father and brothers so much so that when Samuel showed up at the house to anoint the next king, his own father did not even call him in. David's heart had been broken. He'd been rejected by his father and his brothers. He had been disappointed. He had been overlooked and scorned all so that God could be his source.

We know the condition of David's heart by the psalms that he wrote. Psalm 27:10 says, "Some trust in chariots, some in horses, but I will trust in the name of the Lord, my God." David had been through all kinds of hell and that brought him to the realization that the only person he could really depend on was God. So much of David's heart is reflected in the psalms. Read the rest of Psalm 27 and then do your own research into how David's heart had been prepared by all that he had been through.

An Exuberant Declaration of Faith A Psalm of David

The LORD is my light and my salvation;

Whom shall I fear?

The LORD is the strength of my life;

Of whom shall I be afraid?

[2] When the wicked came against me

To eat up my flesh,

My enemies and foes,

They stumbled and fell.

[3] Though an army may encamp against me,

My heart shall not fear;

Though war may rise against me,

In this I will be confident.

[4] One thing I have desired of the LORD,

That will I seek:

That I may dwell in the house of the LORD

All the days of my life,

To behold the beauty of the LORD,

And to inquire in His temple.

5 For in the time of trouble

He shall hide me in His pavilion;

In the secret place of His tabernacle

He shall hide me;

He shall set me high upon a rock.

6 And now my head shall be lifted up above my enemies all around

me;

Therefore I will offer sacrifices of joy in His tabernacle;

I will sing, yes, I will sing praises to the LORD.

7 Hear, O LORD, when I cry with my voice!

Have mercy also upon me, and answer me.

8 When You said, "Seek My face,"

My heart said to You, "Your face, LORD, I will seek."

9 Do not hide Your face from me;

Do not turn Your servant away in anger;

You have been my help;

Do not leave me nor forsake me,

O God of my salvation.

10 When my father and my mother forsake me,

Then the LORD will take care of me.

11 Teach me Your way, O LORD,

And lead me in a smooth path, because of my enemies.

12 Do not deliver me to the will of my adversaries;

For false witnesses have risen against me,

And such as breathe out violence.

[13] I would have lost heart, unless I had believed

That I would see the goodness of the LORD

In the land of the living.

[14] Wait on the LORD;

Be of good courage,

And He shall strengthen your heart;

Wait, I say, on the LORD! (NKJV)

David had truly learned where to place his trust and his heart. His was an action faith in God. He says to wait on the Lord, be of good courage, and allow God to strengthen your heart. That is how you have a heart after God!

You'll never have a heart after God as long as you are looking for people to be your primary source of provision, acknowledge you, and bless you. As long as you are depending upon people, you'll never have a heart after God.

When you think you've got a permanent residence at Heartbreak Hotel, God is trying to get your attention and turn your heart after Him. So, when people walk out on you, when people criticize you, and you're going to serve Him no matter what your situation, you have a heart after God. God is looking for somebody who has a heart after Him.

Key Points:

As long as you are depending upon people you will never have a heart after God.

The truth is people will judge you for your actions not by your intentions.

Proverbs 23:7 says, "For as a man thinketh in his heart, so is he."

God puts a tape measure around your heart not your head.

What's in your heart determines your actions.

You are what is in your heart.

Ask Yourself:

What do I think about most of the time?

Is what's important to God important to me?

Is what burdens God what burdens me?

When He speaks do I listen and do what He says?

Do I change what He wants me to change?

Do I do what He wants me to do?

Do I act like He wants me to act?

Am I looking for people to provide for me, acknowledge me, and bless me?

Declare:

My heart has been broken. I have been let down by people. I have been disappointed by loved ones. I have been rejected, overlooked, and scorned everywhere I turn, but my heart is after God and He is my source and my provider! I desire to think, act, and do what He wants me to do. I will wait on the Lord, be of good courage, and allow Him to strengthen my heart. I want a heart that is after God!

CHAPTER 3

David Possessed a Kingdom Mindset

Not only was David's heart right, not only was he faithful in his assignment, but David also possessed a kingdom mind-set when it came to the Kingdom of God. There are too many of us who think the kingdom of God begins and ends at our doorstep and at our feet. The Kingdom of God is bigger than any one man, bigger than any one woman, and bigger than any one ministry. The Kingdom of God is bigger than you and me.

In order to reign in the Kingdom of God you have to have the right mind-set. Many of us think we are ready to reign, but we are not ready based on our mind-set. When we think about being a king in the Kingdom of God, we view it as an opportunity to be over people, having people serve us or being in charge. We don't realize that we are not just kings; we are what Dr. Myles Munroe calls "servant kings." We've got to understand that greatness in the Kingdom of God is not measured by how many people we have under us, our position, our title or how many letters we have after our name. It is measured by how many people we serve.

The greatness of the McDonald Corporation is not found in how many dollars they have made. When we look at the sign out in front of the restaurants, it tells the public how many billions of people it has served. If we want to know who is great in the Kingdom of God look for the person who has a sign on their heart that says, "I Am a Servant!"

Servant Kings

But Jesus called them to Himself and said to them, "You know those who are considered rulers over the Gentiles lord it over them, and their great ones exercise authority over them. Yet it shall not be so among you; but whoever desires to become great among you shall be your servant. And whoever of you desires to be first shall be slave of all. For even the Son of Man did not come to be served, but to serve, and to give His life a ransom for many. (Mark 10:42-45 NKJV)

Jesus explained this concept of servant leadership to His disciples after the Sons of Thunder, James and John came to Him asking to be allowed to sit on either side of Him when He came into His glory. It is interesting that as Jesus answered their request He told them, "To sit on My right hand and on My left is not Mine to give, but it is for those for whom it is **prepared**" (Mark 10:40 NKJV emphasis added). When the other disciples heard what James and John had requested of Jesus they were understandably upset. Jesus then took that opportunity to explain this concept of servant leadership in the Kingdom of God and compare it to the way the Gentiles rule.

Jesus gave us the definition of servant leadership and how to become great in the Kingdom of God. "Whoever desires to become great among you shall be your servant. And whoever of you desires to be first shall be slave of all." The word servant here is also translated bondservant which means to serve without bondage or one who gives himself up to the will of another, a willing slave.[1] The great Apostle Paul calls himself a bond-servant of Jesus Christ in Romans 1:1.

Jesus also told His disciples that He had and would continue to exemplify servant leadership, "For even the Son of Man did not come to be served, but to serve, and to give His life a ransom for many."

A real servant is interested in seeing that the King gets the glory.

Jesus also exemplified servant leadership when He declared everything, He did was to give glory to His Father.

The words that I speak to you I do not speak on My own authority; but the Father who dwells in Me does the works. (John 14:10 NKJV)

I have glorified You on the earth. I have finished the work which You have given Me to do. (John 17:4 NKJV)

The path to kingship is through learning to serve in obedience and love.

Though He was a Son, He learned obedience by the things which He suffered. And having been perfected, He became the author of eternal salvation to all who obey Him, called by God as High Priest "according to the order of Melchizedek." (Hebrews 5:8-10 NKJV)

David's Ascension to King

He chose David also his servant and took him from the sheepfolds: from following the ewes great with young he brought him to feed Jacob

---

[1] *Vine's Complete Expository Dictionary of Old and New Testament Words,* © 1984, 1996, Thomas Nelson, Inc., Nashville, TN.

his people, and Israel his inheritance. So he fed them according to the integrity of his heart; and guided them by the skillfulness of his hands. (Psalm 78:70-72)

"I have exalted one chosen from the people. I have found David, My servant and with My holy anointing oil I have anointed him." (Psalm 89:19-20 NKJV)

The key to David's ascension to leadership was his servant mind-set. David was a servant. How do we know he was a servant? A real servant is interested in seeing that the King gets the glory. David was always pointing men to praise and glorify God for everything. When he defeated Goliath, he praised God (1 Samuel 17:45-47). When he escaped Saul, he praised God (1 Samuel 24:8-15). When he became king, he gave the glory to God (2 Samuel 5:9). When he brought the Ark back to Israel, he gave the glory to God (2 Samuel 6:21-22). When he fell into sin and got back up, he gave glory to God (Psalm 51). When he got victory in battle, he glorified God (2 Samuel 7:18-29).

A person's mind-set is their state of mind, attitude, outlook, and their way of thinking. It determines their actions, their attitude, and ultimately their altitude. The Bible tells us a prideful or arrogant mind-set leads to our destruction (Proverbs 16:18). An envious or jealous mind-set can actually make a person sick and cause dissention among the people (Proverbs 14:30, 1 Corinthians 3:3). However, the mind-set or attitude of a servant allows God to promote us to a level of leadership. David understood that our attitude must be that of a servant, the same attitude Jesus would later exemplify. Read this paraphrase of Philippians 2:1-11 and meditate on what it means to be Christ-like in leadership.

If you've gotten anything at all out of following Christ, if his love has made any difference in your life, if being in a community of the Spirit means anything to you, if you have a heart, if you care— then do me a favor: Agree with each other, love each other, be deep-spirited friends. Don't push your way to the front; don't sweet-talk your way to the top. Put yourself aside, and help others get ahead. Don't be obsessed with getting your own advantage. Forget yourselves long enough to lend a helping hand.

Think of yourselves the way Christ Jesus thought of himself. He had equal status with God but didn't think so much of himself that he had to cling to the advantages of that status no matter what. Not at all. When the time came, he set aside the privileges of deity and took on the status of a slave, became human! Having become human, he stayed human. It was an incredibly humbling process. He didn't claim special privileges. Instead, he lived a selfless, obedient life and then died a selfless, obedient death—and the worst kind of death at that—a crucifixion.

Because of that obedience, God lifted him high and honored him far beyond anyone or anything, ever, so that all created beings in heaven and on earth—even those long ago dead and buried—will bow in worship before this Jesus Christ and call out in praise that he is the Master of all, to the glorious honor of God the Father. (MSG)

Two Birds and a Frog

The problem with the mind-set nowadays is that everybody wants to get acknowledgment, praise, and credit for everything they do. Everybody wants to point to themselves for having come up with that great idea or brought about a much-needed change or victory in an undesirable situation. What we really need to learn to do as leaders in the Kingdom of God is how to give God the glory for our successes, victories, and achievements. We have a lot of people who are kind of like those in the story about two birds and a frog.

There were two birds and a frog that were in the northern part of the United States and the winter was coming. They realized that the cold weather would soon be upon them, and they needed to get down South where they would be able to survive the winter months. They began to wonder how they could work this out so they could all get safely down South.

The birds said, "Fly."

The frog said, "Hey, brother bird! You can't just leave me here to freeze to death. I've got it. Let's take a stick. One of you can put one end in your claws and the other can put the other end in your claws. I will hold on to the stick with my mouth, and we can all fly down South together."

They took off and everything was going great. Everything was working wonderfully until somebody looked up and said, "WOW! Look at that! Look at those two birds and a frog there. See how the frog is holding on. That's a great idea! Who came up with it?"

The frog said, "I did!" And needless to say, great was his fall. They tell me it wasn't the fall that killed him, but the sudden stop.

He would have made it down South if he wasn't concerned about who got the credit for that great idea.

Serve the Lord with Gladness

God knew that if David could serve a father who had forgotten him, then he could certainly serve a Father who remembered him in his low estate. David served the Lord with gladness because God had prepared him to reign! When the time came for David to ascend to the throne, he had learned to be faithful in whatever he was doing. His heart and his mind-set were focused on the Kingdom of God, not self-serving or self-centered. David was ready to be a servant king!

Serve the LORD with gladness; Come before His presence with singing. (Psalm 100:2 NKJV)

Key Points:

David served the Lord with gladness because God had prepared him to reign.

Whoever desires to become great among you shall be a servant to all.

A real servant is interested in seeing that the King gets the glory.

And whoever of you desires to be first shall be slave of all.

Put yourself aside and try to help others get ahead.

Don't try to push your way to the front.

Serve the Lord with gladness.

Be a servant-leader.

Ask Yourself:

Do I attempt to agree with others or do I need my own way?

Do I try and push my way to the front or do I allow God to promote me?

Do I try to sweet-talk my way to the top to avoid the preparation process?

Do I put myself aside, and help others get ahead?

Am I obsessed with getting my own way?

Am I able to forget myself long enough to lend a helping hand?

Declare:

My desire is to become great in the Kingdom of God so I shall be a bondservant for Him. May everything I do give glory to God no matter where I find myself. May I continually serve the Lord with gladness in my heart and a servant-leader mind-set.

SECTION TWO

Jesse

It is a wonderful thing and a blessing to know that God loves us enough to have someone there to help make up for the pain and the agony we experience when we are rejected and overlooked by those who are supposed to embrace us and make us feel loved and protected. God is so concerned with our development that He sends someone to serve as a surrogate or a substitute to be that catalyst for us on the road to our destiny.

The Father Who Overlooked Me

Thus, Jesse made seven of his sons pass before Samuel. And Samuel said to Jesse, "The Lord has not chosen these." And Samuel said to Jesse, "Are all the young men here?" Then he said, "There remains yet the youngest, and there he is, keeping the sheep." And Samuel said to Jesse, "Send and bring him. For we will not sit down till he comes here." (1 Samuel 16:10-11 NKJV)

If I had a choice today between being overlooked or being forgotten, I would probably choose to be forgotten. To be forgotten means that for one reason or another the very thought of me did not enter your mind. Perhaps it can be written off as a memory lapse or a temporary glitch in your mind's computer that caused you to fail to be able to pull up my file that is somewhere between your ears. However, to be overlooked has within it implications that make that experience much more painful than being forgotten. According to the Webster's New World Dictionary, to be overlooked means to "look beyond and not to see." It means to "fail to notice" or worse than that, "to ignore or pass over indulgently or with desire."

According to this definition, when someone overlooks you they did not do it by mistake. It was intentional! They saw you. They looked at you. They knew of your talents, your skills, your gifts, and they even knew that you were qualified, but decided for one reason or another that they did not want to choose you. Perhaps in their mind they felt that you were not on their wish list. Maybe they felt that you did not align with their group or come under their area of control, you were not the kind of person they wanted to deal with in spite of your ability. Maybe the system in which they were functioning was filled with racism and prejudice, so you were not chosen based upon the color of your skin or the country of your birth. Maybe in their eyes you did not have the right last name or the right political party affiliation. Maybe they were making their decisions based on politics and favoritism.

There is something very painful about being overlooked. What is even more painful is when the person who overlooked you is supposed to be in the capacity of a father. When we speak of a father, we speak of that person who is the agent of birthing and nurturing. He is the one who is supposed to be endorsing you, promoting you, and ensuring that you soar to majestic heights as you pursue your destiny in God. Instead of that person endorsing you and blessing you, they strangely turn against you and decide to ignore you, oppress you, belittle you, and tear down the very confidence that they are supposed to build in you. The jagged knife of rejection, the piercing darts of disregard, and the staggering blows of scorn are all inflicted upon the soul by the person that you seem to need the most. For some reason they have decided to overlook you.

David, Son of Jesse

I find it strange and even sad that when one is in their days of small beginnings there are few that want to take interest in them or take the time to pour into them. But after destiny has unfolded and greatness has been achieved, many of the same people who despised and rejected them will, all of a sudden, attempt to line up and want to take credit for their success. When I looked at this, I wonder who would not want to be associated with David, the greatest of Israel's kings. Who would not want to stand and boast that they knew him before he was the king, and claim they were one of the ones to first see that flicker of potential that would grow into a forest fire of success? Believe it or not, like most successful people, while David was in his time of humble beginnings, he had very few who would stamp their seal of approval upon him. Unfortunately, that included his father, Jesse.

Many places throughout Scripture David is identified as the son of Jesse. Jesse was the son of Boaz and Ruth whose story is recorded in the

Book of Ruth. Although Jesse was of prominent lineage, he was un-known and of a modest station in life. We know that Jesse had eight sons, the youngest of whom was David. Jesse's wealth consisted chiefly of sheep for which David acted as shepherd. The name "Jesse" means "doubtful" but it also means "wealthy" and "Yahweh Exists." However, for David his father's name would always be associated with the one who overlooked him.

When the prophet Samuel showed up at the house of Jesse, sent by God to anoint the next king, this father thought it was not worthwhile to call David into the room to attend the Anointing Ceremony! He simply overlooked him.

The question then becomes, what do you do when someone who is supposed to endorse you and support you decides to overlook you? In order to overcome being overlooked the thing to do is: Look Up! Look In! Look On!

CHAPTER 4

When Overlooked, Look Up!

My voice shalt thou hear in the morning, O LORD; in the morning will I direct my prayer unto thee and will look up. (Psalm 5:3)

Now symbolically speaking, "Look Up" symbolizes expectation and hope. It is the eye of the spirit man fastening upon God with utter dependence and need. As a matter of fact, I found out that the word for "man" is the Greek word *anthropos*, which actually has the connotations of "one who looks up." You have not become that man or woman that God has called you to be until you learn to "look up." I know that society is trying to tell you that you're supposed to be independent. However, the real man/ woman recognizes his/her limitations and realizes that without God he can do nothing.

We need to understand that as painful as rejection and oversight is God has a purpose in allowing it to happen. Each episode of oversight and rejection is designed to actually build our relationship with God. The God we serve is sovereign and He is in control. He reigns and super-reigns. He rules and super-rules. God brings us into contact with people who are going to connect with our vision and connect with our spirit. We call these Divine Appointments and Divine Connections.

Not only does God provide Divine Appointments and Divine Connections, He also allows Divine Exits. God allows people to leave us and walk out of our lives in order that He might fulfill a larger purpose. We love Divine Appointments! We love Divine Connections! There are some people that come into our lives who seem to provide a certain amount of comfort, a certain amount of love, and a certain amount of fellowship for us. But there are times when God will tap a person on the shoulder and say, "Listen, it's time for you to get out of their life." We do not like to deal with that kind of thing. God sometimes allows certain people to reject us, overlook us, and walk out of our lives in order that He may fulfill a larger purpose. What God desires is that we have enough trust in Him to say, "God, I do not want people in my life that You do not want in my life. If You decide that they're going to walk away, I'm going to trust that You do everything to fulfill Your purpose in my life. I trust you, God with my life and my relationships!"

You ought to thank God for Divine Exits.

When God allows people to walk out of our lives it is because He is getting us ready for something greater. It is part of our preparation to reign in His Kingdom. You ought to thank God for Divine Exits. God has got a bigger plan. He's got something greater for you.

New Beginnings

And the Lord said unto Samuel, How long will you mourn for Saul seeing that I have rejected him from reigning over Israel? Fill thing horn with oil and go, and I will send thee to Jesse the Bethlehemite, for I have provided me a king among his sons. (1 Samuel 16:1)

God instructed Samuel to go to the house of Jesse. When he gets there, Jesse brings in his seven sons. The number seven is significant in the Bible because it is the number of completions. Jesse thought he already had his completion. In the eyes of Jesse, David represented an unexpected birth, he's number eight which actually means "new beginnings." But instead of seeing David as a new beginning, Jesse sees him as a mistake and did not value him. Therefore, all Jesse's seven sons pass before Samuel except David.

Then Samuel said to Jesse, "The Lord had not chosen these. Are these all of your children?" Jesse answered, "Well, there's David, the youngest, he is keeping the sheep" (1 Samuel 16:9-11).

David, the youngest, the mistake, the overlooked one is out doing the job no one else wanted to do. His father does not even recognize him. The father who was supposed to be endorsing David did not even call him into the room. He did not even think it was worthwhile. His father valued all the other sons, but he looked upon David as a mistake and the least likely to be chosen as king.

God chose David in spite of the fact that his father did not recognize him, in spite of the fact that nobody liked him. His brothers should have stepped up and said, "Hey, dad. Wait a minute. You forgot about David." Not even his brothers would recognize him, but God chose him!

For promotion cometh neither from the east nor from the west, nor from the south. But God is the judge: he putteth down one and setteth up another. (Psalm 75:6-7)

God's got a purpose for you so you should be looking up in expectation!

God used the rejection of his father and his brothers to create in David a desire to be in the presence of God. "Nobody else accepts me so while I'm out here watching the sheep all by myself, I'm going to get in the presence of Almighty God." Do you know that there is a place where you are fully accepted, where you are fully understood? Some of us will not get to that place until we get overlooked, until some people walk out of our lives, and we finally go running into the presence of God. In the presence of the Lord there is fullness of joy. There are some things that we cannot get from human relationships. There are some things that we cannot get from a spouse, sons, daughters or from the family of God.

When you are rejected and overlooked, there is a daddy that welcomes you into His presence. He understands you when others misunderstand you. He loves you when others hate you. When your earthly father rejects you, your Heavenly Father accepts you. He loves you just the way you are!

When your earthly father rejects you, your Heavenly Father accepts you.

Read all of Psalm 27 but particularly notice Psalm 27:10. "When my father and my mother forsake me, then the Lord will take care of me" (NKJV). David is in the field where nobody was even thinking about him. This is where David made a lot of declarations about his relationship with his Heavenly Father. In Psalm 121:1-2 David said," I will lift up mine eyes from whence cometh my help. My help cometh from the Lord, which made the heaven and the earth."

David knew the answers he sought for his life could only be found in looking up. In Psalm 123:1-2 he declared, "Unto thee lift I up mine eyes, O Thou that dwellest in the heavens. Behold, as the eyes of servants look unto the hand of their masters, and as the eyes of the maiden unto the hand of the mistress; so our eyes wait upon the Lord our God, until that he have mercy upon us.

After he had been rejected, David realized where his help came from and he cried out, "Hear, O Israel, if it had not been for the Lord when men rose up against us, then they had swallowed us up quick, when their wrath was kindled against us" (Psalm 124:2-3). Then in verse 8 he added, "Our help is in the name of the Lord, who made heaven and earth" (NKJV).

It's time to Look Up! You have been depending on man too long. You have been looking at people too long! It's time to look up. They have overlooked you and rejected you because God wants your attention. It's time to look up because God's got a greater plan for you.

You have been depending on man and looking at people too long! It's time to look up!

Key Points:

When your earthly father rejects you, your Heavenly Father accepts you.

You've been depending on man and looking at people too long!

Thank God for Divine Connections **and** Divine Exits.

Realize your help comes only from the Lord.

God's got a specific purpose for you.

It's time to look up!

Ask Yourself:

Can I say, I do not want people in my life that God doesn't want in my life?

If people walk away, reject, or overlook me can I trust God with my life?

Can I trust God to fulfill His purpose in my life?

Will I look to Him for my help and not to others?

Can I receive God's love even though my own earthly parents have rejected me?

Declare:

Whether others like me or not, I know that I am chosen by God to fulfill a specific purpose with my life. I know that in God's own time He is going to elevate me to my place of assignment whether others see it or not. I am looking up! I will lift up my eyes unto the hills because like David, I know that that is where my help comes from!

CHAPTER 5

When Overlooked, Look In

The most important question that each of us must answer in life is, Who Are we? What is our purpose and why are we here? I would never follow anyone who does not know who they are, and neither would I follow some whose very existence is wrapped up in someone else. If I'm going to follow someone, they have to possess an understanding of who they are. The search for self begins with a knowledge of who has you. Look In and understand how you were created and whose you are.

Have you had something break that was beyond your ability to repair it – a car or an appliance? Usually when that happens, you have to do one of two things. You take it to someone who knows how to fix it or take it to the manufacturer because the one who made it knows how to fix it.

Therefore, after one **Looks Up** one must **Look In.** In looking in we must ask ourselves, who has created me and who do I belong to. When I find Him, I will know who I am. Look at how the Psalmist put it in Psalm 8:1-4.

What is man that thou art mindful of him: or the son of man, that thou visitest him? For thou hast made him a little lower than the angels, and hast crowned him with glory and honor. Thou madest him to have dominion over the works of thy hands; thou hast put all things under his feet.

Who Am I?

I will praise thee; for I am fearfully and wonderfully made: marvelous are thy works; and that my soul knoweth right well. (Psalm 139:14)

David discovered who he was. Do you know who you are? You might be white, almost white, honey brown or triple chocolate, but you are fearfully and wonderfully made. Thin, wide, short or tall, you are fearfully and wonderfully made. Short hair, red hair, black hair, brown hair, dyed hair or nappy hair, you are fearfully and wonderfully made. You might be smart or not so smart or somewhere in between, but you are fearfully and wonderfully made. Are you eloquent, loud, quiet, emotional, still, happy, introverted, or extroverted? Makes no difference, you are still fearfully and wonderfully made. You need to have an understanding of who you are, but it is not based upon what other people are telling you. It is based upon who your God is and what He made you to be.

When we know who we are we possess within us the ability to turn the tables on being overlooked!

If you will take the time to search out the Scriptures, you will find out exactly who God says you are. God spoke through the prophet Moses in Deuteronomy 28:13, "And the LORD will make you the head and not the tail; you shall be above only, and not be beneath" (NKJV),

The Apostle Peter said, "But you *are* a chosen generation, a royal priesthood, a holy nation, His own special people, that you may proclaim the praises of Him who called you out of darkness into His marvelous light" (1 Peter 2:9 NKJV). God has crowned you with glory and honor.

God chose you before the foundation of the earth (Ephesians 1:4). No one has a right to tell you who you are because God has already told you who you are. You are somebody.

Now much of our consternation in life about who we are happens when people overlook us or even do things to us. Being overlooked can be taken as an attack on our self-image if we don't know who we are. But when we know who we are we possess within us the ability to turn the tables on being overlooked. We can walk out after they have overlooked us and say, "That company just missed out on the best employee they could have ever hired." We can tell that guy or girl who walked out on us that they just missed out on a blessing. We can tell that church that decided to hire another pastor that they just missed out on the greatest pastor they could have ever had.

When you know who you are, being overlooked isn't going to kill you because you can flip the switch and turn the tables. You know that you are of value and will be a blessing to anything to which you get attached. You know who you are in God and know that if you become a part of something, it's going to get better than it ever was before you were there.

We've got to know who we are in God.

Is that being conceited? No! That is being confident in the God that we serve and His ability to work in our life. We have to believe in ourselves. If we walk into a company, we have to believe that it's going to be better because we are there. We've got to walk into a ministry believing it's going to be a better ministry because we are there. When we enter a relationship, we have to believe that whatever they were before, they are going to be all that and a whole lot more because we are with them. We've got to know who we are in God.

Who Should I Listen to?

Blessed is the man who walks not in the counsel of the ungodly, nor stands in the path of sinners, nor sits in the seat of the scornful; But his delight is in the law of the Lord, and in His law he meditates day and night. He shall be like a tree planted by the rivers of water, that brings forth its fruit in its season, whose leaf also shall not wither; and whatever he does shall prosper. (Psalm 1:1-3 NKJV)

We all have a choice who we will listen to. Who will you choose to listen to? Will it be the father who has rejected you or the Holy Spirit who says you are a child of God? (Romans 8:16)

Are you going to listen to the lover who spurned you or God who says He loves you with an everlasting love? (Psalm 52:8)

Are you going to listen to the parent or family member that abused you, that abusive spouse that battered you or God who says you are precious in His sight? (Psalm 116:15)

Are you going to listen to the abusive minister who belittled you or God who says you are called to rule and reign in His Kingdom? (Revelation 20:6)

Are you going to listen to the commercial that tries to tell you that you are too black and too fat or to God who says He we are all equal in His eyes? (Romans 10:12)

Are you listening to the educator that is trying to tell you that you are too dumb to learn or God who says you have the mind of Christ? (1 Corinthians 2:16)

You've got to decide who you are going to listen!

David had to deal with an episode in his life where he had been overlooked. David had to make a choice because there were actually two or three voices that were speaking to him by their actions. His father and his brothers basically told him that he was worthless. Samuel, on the other hand, said God had chosen him as the next King of Israel. He had to decide who he was going to listen to. David had already spent time preparing for this moment. He may not have known he was about to be anointed as the next king of Israel, but he had no doubt that God had plans for him.

Samuel knew the minute David walked into the room that this was the man he was to anoint. Everyone else may have rejected him, but God said this is the one!

And the LORD said, "Arise, anoint him; for this is the one!" Then Samuel took the horn of oil and anointed him in the midst of his brothers; and the Spirit of the LORD came upon David from that day forward. (1 Samuel 16:12-13 NKJV)

Being overlooked by his father Jesse could have had an extremely damaging effect upon David, especially when one considers the role of the Hebrew father. In those days the father of the Hebrew home was the one from whom the sons received their identity. Back then, papa was more than just a baby's daddy. He was the person who possessed "naming rights." Naming rights carried the power to speak destiny over that child. It was the father who named his sons. Hebrew names were very important for they spoke of the destiny of that child.

For a father to not even call his son into the room when an honored visitor was there basically meant this boy did not even exist in the mind of that father. This could have killed David, but he had spent time in preparation with his Heavenly Father and he knew who he was. The rest of his life David had the pain that many of us experience today of wearing somebody's name who did not endorse him.

David, the son of Jesse; he had to wear the name of a father who did not even accept him. He realized that he did not have to possess the spirit of the one whose name he carried. Just because his earthly father was not a good father to him did not mean that David was not capable of being a good father. Just because your daddy ran off and left his family does not mean that you've got to run off and leave your family. You may have the name but that does not mean that you have to bear the character. You might have the name of your earthly father but you can have the character of your Heavenly Father. Maybe your daddy gave you a bad name. Maybe your daddy overlooked you. Maybe your mother, your brothers, your sisters, and friends overlooked you. You can attach yourself to your Heavenly Father and walk in victory knowing that He has anointed you for such a time as this.

Key Points:

Within us is the ability to turn the tables on being overlooked and rejected.

God has His eyes on each of us and has chosen us for His purpose.

We are to listen only to the voice of Almighty God.

We aren't to let anyone else tell us who we are.

We've got to know who we are in God.

We are who God says we are!

We are the chosen ones!

We are anointed!

Ask Yourself:

Who am I listening to?

Am I listening to a parent who has rejected me?

Am I listening to the lover who spurned me?

Am I listening to the person who abused me?

Am I listening to a boss or a leader who belittles me?

Am I listening to the commercial that tries to tell me what I should look like?

Am I listening to the educator that tells me I am too dumb?

Am I listening to my Creator who has chosen and anointed me for such a time as this?

Declare:

I've decided that I'm going to listen to the voice of Almighty God. I'm not going to let anyone else tell me who I am. I know who I am and it is based upon the Word of the Living God. I am who God says I am! The One who made me says I am His so it does not make any difference what anyone else has to say. My Creator has chosen and anointed me for such a time as this!

CHAPTER 6

When Overlooked, Look On

So Samuel took the horn of oil and anointed him in the presence of his brothers, and from that day on the Spirit of the LORD came powerfully upon David. (1 Samuel 16:13 NIV)

When overlooked we are to Look Up because God is our source, not anyone or anything on this earth! Our power, provision, and strength come from our Heavenly Father. When we are overlooked, we are to Look In because we are who our Creator says we are, not who others say we are! Our name and our identity come from our Heavenly Father. Once we get a grip on who we are then we need to understand that we are going somewhere. When overlooked we are to Look On! We are to look ahead to the future! In spite of the fact that his father overlooked him, David received what God had for him through the prophet Samuel. He looked toward the future.

God will call you a king while you are still a kid.
Futuristic Anointing

David receives what I call a "futuristic anointing." He was not anointed just for where he was at the moment. He was anointed for where he was going. This is strange because God called David a king while he is still a kid. God does strange things like that. He will call you prosperous while you are still broke. He will call you blessed when you are still down. He will call you a millionaire when you're not even a "thousandaire." He'll call you delivered while you are still bound. He'll call you a diamond when you are still in the rough. He will call you a king while you are still a kid.

Though Samuel anointed David as the next king, only David and his family knew about this. It was done in secret. In other words, God was telling David, I have a plan for your life. However, that did not mean David was to go out and tell everyone he was going to be the next king. David still had training to go through before he was fit to reign as the true servant-leader of God's people. There was more to the preparation process that David was going to have to go through.

Though David was anointed to take Saul's place, he was now called to go serve under King Saul in his palace. Notice that is says in I Samuel 16:14, "But the Spirit of the Lord departed from Saul, and a distressing spirit from the Lord troubled him" (NIV). King Saul would fly off into fits of rage. David was called to play his harp to soothe King Saul when this distressing spirit came upon him.

It is interesting to note here that one of King Saul's servants was used by the Lord to bring David into the palace for his next level of training. This servant obvious knew something about David that had been kept secret since Samuel had anointed him.

Then one of the servants answered and said, "Look, I have seen a son of Jesse the Bethlehemite, who is skillful in playing, a mighty man of valor, a man of war, prudent in speech, and a handsome person; and the LORD is with him." Therefore, Saul sent messengers to Jesse, and said, "Send me your son David, who is with the sheep." (1 Samuel 16:18-19 NKJV)

This servant said to King Saul, "The Lord is with David, this lowly shepherd boy." It is also interesting that although King Saul knew David was the son of Jesse and was out doing the despicable job of tending the sheep, he sent for the boy because the servant told him the Lord was with David. We also read that during this time David went back and forth between working at the palace where he served King Saul and Jesse's house where he continued to care for the sheep. His responsibilities at home may have even increased because the Bible tells us that his three older brothers joined Saul's army.

During this time David also comes to face the Philistine giant, Goliath. His father sent him to Saul's army camp, not as a soldier but as a delivery boy. Once again, his father is overlooking even what he knows the Prophet Samuel has said about David. As David speaks with the soldiers, he hears the challenge put forth by Goliath. Once again, his brothers belittle him and tell him he should stop being so conceited and return to the sheepfold where he belongs (1 Samuel 17:17-29). When King Saul hears David is in the camp, he calls for him. When David offers to go before the giant, King Saul rejects the offer saying he is too young and too untrained to face such a seasoned warrior.

David explains that he understands that the reason God had him in the fields as a shepherd was to prepare him for such a time as this. Even in the fields with the sheep, David was looking to the future. He knew God was training him to be a king. Now he can say to King Saul, "The Lord who delivered me from the paw of the lion and from the paw of the bear; He will deliver me from the hand of the Philistine" (1 Samuel 17:37 NKJV). David had looked up and seen God as His source, he had looked in and knew who God said he was to be, and he looked ahead knowing God would give him the victory and use it to show them all that the battle was the Lord's (1 Samuel 17:46-47).

After the victory over Goliath the Bible says, "David went out wherever Saul sent him, and behaved wisely. And Saul set him over the men of war, and he was accepted in the sight of all the people and also in the sight of Saul's servants" (1 Samuel 18:13-14). David was in training for reigning. He behaved wisely looking to the future as God prepared him for ascension to the throne.

From the Palace to the Cave

David's favor in King Saul's court was short-lived, however. Once God felt David had learned all he could in this position, He moved David on to the next level of preparation. Though David behaved wisely, he eventually had to run for his life to escape the accusations and attacks against him by King Saul. It appears that King Saul found out David was to be the next king because he told Jonathan that he would never be king if he did not kill David (1 Samuel 20:30-31). David was now a fugitive having been wrongly accused of conspiring against the king, but it was all part of God's plan. It was all part of God's preparing David to reign.

David had to spend time in the Cave of Adullam as a fugitive. His army now consisted of all those who were in distress, in debt, and discontented. There were about four hundred men with him (1 Samuel 22:1-2). David was no longer shepherding sheep, now he was caring for an army of misfits and malcontents. David was at a time in his life when he had to become totally dependent on the Lord. Every time he faced a battle or a difficult situation, he asked the Lord for direction. Though it appeared he was wandering around in the wilderness, he knew God had a plan and a purpose for his life. He was looking to the future even those his present conditions looked nothing like a palace.

Beware of what seems like perfect opportunities to "help God" fulfill the prophecy that has been spoken over you.

Twice David had the opportunity to "help God along" with what he knew God had called him to be. He knew Samuel had anointed him to be the next king. He knew Saul was the only thing standing in his way. He could have become impatient and tried to help God out by killing Saul. Twice he had the opportunity to kill Saul. Even David's own men thought he was foolish for not taking advantage of what seemed like perfect opportunities to move forward and fulfill the prophecy over him. David had a choice to make. God was building character and integrity in David to prepare him to reign.

But David said to Abishai, "Do not destroy him; for who can stretch out his hand against the LORD's anointed, and be guiltless?" David said furthermore, "As the LORD lives, the LORD shall strike him, or his day shall come to die, or he shall go out to battle and perish. The LORD forbid that I should stretch out my hand against the LORD's anointed. But please, take now the spear and the jug of water that are by his head, and let us go." (1 Samuel 26:9-11 NKJV)

David had still more steps to complete in this process toward his future, but he faithfully kept his eyes on the goal set before him as the Apostle Paul was later to write in Philippians 3:13-14.

Brethren, I do not count myself to have apprehended; but one thing I do, forgetting those things which are behind and reaching forward to those things which are ahead, I press toward the goal for the prize of the upward call of God in Christ Jesus. (NKJV)

God's Plans to Prosper You

"For I know the plans I have for you," declares the Lord, "plans to prosper you and not to harm you, plans to give you hope and a future." (Jeremiah 29:11 NIV)

God has plans to prosper you and not to harm you. His plans for you are to give you hope and a future. This means "intentions, purpose, and inventions." In other words God says, "I know the plans that I have for you when I invented you." You plans that you will be blessed, that you will prosper, and that you will be successful at what He has called you to do with your life. You need to realize that God has plans that you will be blessed. He knew you in your mother's womb and has had a plan for you since the very beginning. When God has a plan that means He has a purpose for your life. When God has a plan and a purpose for your life that means He has already made provision for you to accomplish that plan and that purpose.

David realized that even though he had been anointed by Samuel as the next king, he had to go back to the sheepfold and continue to serve his earthly father as his Heavenly Father put His plan to work. What David had to do though is keep in the back of his mind, "I'm going to be king! I have been chosen and anointed by God to do this!" He was out there shearing the sheep but he was saying, "I'm going to be king!" While he was out there protecting the sheep in the wind and the rain, he was talking to himself saying, "I'm going to be king."

This means that while you are sweeping the floor you've got to look at yourself and say that one day somebody's going to sweep the floor for me. While you are out flipping burgers and saying, "Welcome to McDonalds" you've got to talk to yourself and say, "One day I'm going to be the manager." You have got to be in the mail room saying, "This is just a step in the process because one day I'm going to be the CEO! I'm Looking On! I'm looking toward the future! I am looking toward an expected end."

Your future is bright. You may not be there yet but you know in God's own time He's going to take you to that place. Know that your future is in the hands of Almighty God. Know that your future might be in the sheepfold right now but in God's own time He is going to take you to your place. You may be down and out right now but that's alright. As long as God is on the throne you know He holds the future in His hand. Get ready! Your future is bright! It's time to **Look On!**

Eye hath not seen, nor ear heard, neither have entered into the heart of man, the things that God hath prepared for them that love him. (1 Corinthians 2:9)

Key Points:
Beware of what seem like perfect opportunities to help God out.
He has already made provision to accomplish His purpose.
He will call you a king while you are still a kid.
God has a plan and a purpose for your life.
God's taking you to your place.
Your future is bright!
Look ahead!

Look on!

Ask Yourself:
Am I looking toward the future?
Am I am looking toward an expected end?
Do I see a bright future ahead of me?
Do I believe God is going to take me to that place?
Am I confident that my future is in the hands of Almighty God?

Declare:
God's got a blessing for me down the road. If I just keep on living like God wants me to, one day I am going to be everything that God wants me to be. I know that even though I might be in the sheepfold right now, in God's own time He is going to take me to my place. As long as God is on the throne, I know He holds the future in His hand. I am ready! I'm Looking On! I'm looking toward the future! I am looking toward an expected end!

SECTION THREE

Samuel

God, in His wisdom, manages our affairs in such a way that for every father like Jesse who overlooks us, He provides a Samuel who is there to lay hands on us to affirm us or to endorse us. An endorsement is a powerful thing. It serves as a recommendation that reflects upon the person being endorsed, but more so reflects upon the person doing the endorsing. The endorser basically stamps his hand of approval upon the endorsee.

The Prophet Who Laid Hands on Me

And Samuel grew, and the LORD was with him, and did let none of his words fall to the ground. And all Israel from Dan even to Beersheba knew that Samuel was established to be a prophet of the LORD. (1 Samuel 3:19-20 NKJV)

It is important to choose someone of power to endorse you because an endorsement is a very powerful thing. It serves as a recommendation that reflects upon the person being endorsed as well as the one making the endorsement. The endorser is throwing the weight of his experience and power behind that individual. He is setting him forth with the full weight of his ability to discern and to detect potential for greatness. There are even times when he is saying that this person is somewhat of a replica of who I am, and I have poured myself into him or her. Now he or she possesses my spiritual DNA. So, whether you are called to the secular arena or called to the Church world, let me say that the best thing that you can do is to find somebody who is great at what they do and have that individual endorse you. Find someone who is willing to lay their hands upon you.

When it comes to this, I find myself extremely thankful to God for the fact that for every Jesse who overlooks me, God has a Samuel that He sends to lay hands upon me. For everyone who rejects me there is someone who God uses to notice me. For everyone who speaks against me, thank God, there is someone who speaks for me. I believe that it is important that we recognized the awesome ability of our God to balance those types of experiences in our lives.

If everybody overlooked me all the time, my self-image and my self-esteem would be torn down to a point that I could never have had the confidence to go forward and do what God has called me to do. On the other hand, if everyone accepted me and refused to reject me at any time than I would suffer from a case of "Big Head Syndrome "and be so filled with pride that I would never feel the need to seek the face of God or even to serve Him for that matter.

So, God, in His wisdom, allows a delicate mixture of bitterness and sweetness, of acceptance and rejection, of denigration and celebration. We need someone to lift us up and someone to down us; somebody to encourage us and somebody to discourage us; somebody to be for us and somebody to be against us. We need to understand that all of these individuals are simply a part of the drama that is called "Life." That's why we don't need to get overly uptight or upset at the comings and goings of individuals in our lives.

We don't need to over-emphasize whether others reject us or accept us. We don't need to get uptight or upset when people walk in or out of our lives. Everybody who comes into my life is simply a part of the drama. They are individuals under the control of the hand of the puppet master who is working out His will in their life and our lives. We need to understand that God uses each and every individual to help build us into what He needs us to be. Stay tuned while the drama unfolds!

We need someone to lift us up and someone to down us; somebody to encourage us and somebody to discourage us; somebody to be for us and somebody to be against us.

You don't need to set aside the book before the next chapter is revealed. You don't need to walk away while you're still down in the valley. You don't need to give up and throw in the towel. You need to hang in there until the drama unfolds. It's not over until God says it's over!

All things work together for good to those that love God and who are the called according to His purpose. (Romans 8:28)

Samuel, the Prophet

An extremely important character stepped on to the stage of David's life, sent by God to shape and mold him. This character is a man that we have come to know as Samuel, the prophet. If ever there was a time when Israel needed a man like Samuel, it was during this moment of their history.

G. Frederick Owens, in his book entitled "Abraham to the Middle East," described this time in Israel's history as a time when the people were backslidden and very far away from God. There was corruption and idol worship throughout the land. The hearts of the people were far away from serving the true and living God of Israel. It was a dark time in which the Bible says every man did what was right in his own eyes. 1 Samuel 3:1 says that there were not many visions, so no one spoke for God and no one sought the face of God. On top of that, Eli, the backslidden priest and his sons, had corrupted the temple which much to the displeasure of God had nullified and silenced the voice of the Church. It was during this crisis hour that God raised up a voice to speak relief to crisis and answers to questions. That man was a man by the name of Samuel.

The story of Samuel's life reads like an action novel.

Mark A. Tabb in his book entitled, "Heroes of the Faith," wrote that the story of Samuel's life "reads like an action novel." He was a man of God at a time when such men were short in supply. Samuel never backed down from a challenge and his faith kept him from being intimidated by anyone regardless of the person's position. It was because of the type of man that he was that God would speak to him to be the one person who would come and lay his hands upon the man who would be not only the next King of Israel, but the greatest king that Israel would ever have. Samuel would lay hands on the man that would rise up to be one of the most significant figures in biblical as well as world history.

What was it that God saw in this man Samuel? What kind of person should I look for to lay hands upon me? There are some characteristics that Samuel had that I believe can be applied when we are searching for someone to lay hands on us.

CHAPTER 7

Someone Who Hears the Voice of God

The first characteristic that Samuel the prophet exhibited is that he heard the **Voice of God**. We are living in a time and a day in which there seems to be a lot of confusion regarding the voice of God. As a matter of fact, we are having a hard time today distinguishing between the **Voice of God**, the **Voice of the Devil**, and the **Voice of Self**. We see things happening in the Church where people think that they are hearing the Voice of God, but based upon their actions we recognize that they are hearing a different voice. We had one preacher appeared on television claiming God told him that He was going to kill him if he did not raise a certain amount of money. We heard another preacher tell us God told him to leave his wife and be married to the ministry. Then this same man married someone else a week after his divorce was final. We had another preacher on TV claiming that God told him that unless "you belong to a certain political party you cannot be a Christian." People are confusing the Voice of God with the Voice of the Devil and their own desires which is the Voice of Self.

Samuel Knew the Voice of God

And the Lord came, and stood, and called as at other times, Samuel, Samuel. Then Samuel answered, Speak; for thy servant heareth. And the Lord said to Samuel, Behold, I will do a thing in Israel, at which both the ears of everyone that heareth it shall tingle. (1 Samuel 3:10-11)

The thing that made Samuel a man of God was he learned to hear the Voice of God from a very young age. When we look at 1 Samuel 3:1 we find there the story of a young man who is just six years old. Don't let anybody try to convince you that you have to wait until your child is older to let him make a decision concerning Christ. You can raise a child that can be in tune to hear the voice of Almighty God from a very young age.

Now the boy Samuel ministered to the Lord before Eli. And the word of the Lord was rare in those days; there was no widespread revelation. And it came to pass at that time, while Eli was lying down in his place, and when his eyes had begun to grow so dim that he could not see, and before the lamp of God went out in the tabernacle of the Lord where the ark of God was, and while Samuel was lying down, that the Lord called Samuel. And he answered, "Here I am!" So he ran to Eli and said, "Here I am, for you called me." And he said, "I did not call; lie down again." And he went and lay down. (1 Samuel 3:1-5 NKJV)

This is interesting because Samuel hears the Voice of God in the midst of a corrupt priesthood. If you look at the Scripture just a few verses before this, he had actually been in the presence of Eli when he was talking about his sons who had corrupted the kingdom. They had corrupted the priesthood. These young men were engaged in all kinds of acts. When Samuel hears the voice of God, he does what we do many times and went back to a system, even a corrupt one, to ask whether or not it was God.

Then the LORD called yet again, "Samuel!" So Samuel arose and went to Eli, and said, "Here I am, for you called me." He answered, "I did not call, my son; lie down again." (Now Samuel did not yet know the

LORD, nor was the word of the LORD yet revealed to him.) And the LORD called Samuel again the third time. So he arose and went to Eli, and said, "Here I am, for you did call me." Then Eli perceived that the LORD had called the boy. (1 Samuel 3:6-8 NKJV)

Notice it says, "Samuel did not yet know the Lord, nor was the word of the Lord yet revealed to him." Fortunately, Eli had not gotten so far away from God that when Samuel asks him this question for the third time he recognized that God was speaking to Samuel. He said, "Go, lie down; and it shall be, if He calls you, that you must say, 'Speak, Lord, for Your servant hears'" (1 Samuel 3:9). At six years old, this young man learned what it meant to hear the voice of God. In 1 Samuel 3:10-14, God reveals His plan to this young boy.

In 1 Samuel 3:19-20 it says, "And Samuel grew, and the LORD was with him, and did let none of his words fall to the ground. And all Israel from Dan even to Beersheba knew that Samuel was established to be a prophet of the LORD." From that time on, God knew that He had some-one to whom He could speak, who could discern His Voice, and would be obedient to what He had to say. From that time on, Samuel was a man who was recognized by God, and recognized in the land as some-body who could hear the voice of Almighty God.

God knew that when He was ready to anoint another king after Saul, there was somebody who would hear what He had to say. In I Samuel 16:1 the Lord said to Samuel, "How long will you mourn for Saul, seeing I have rejected him from reigning over Israel? Fill your horn with oil and go; I am sending you to Jesse the Bethlehemite. For I have provided Myself a king among his sons" (NKJV).

Samuel had such a relationship with God that he told Him he was afraid for if King Saul heard about it he would kill him. God had asked Samuel to deal with his emotions so he could move forward in God's plan. Samuel was mourning over the loss of Saul's favor with God. We know at this point that Saul was not yet dead because Samuel admitted he feared Saul would come after him and kill him. Sometimes we allow our emotions to get in the way of hearing God's voice and following God's plan.

I have learned as a pastor that I can't lead by my emotions. I can't promote people just because I like them. I have to be able to discern between my own emotions and what God wants and what God is saying. We cannot live our lives based upon our emotions because our emotions are going to fluctuate. One day we're happy and the next day we're sad. We've got to get to a point where we are disciplined enough say, "God, not my will but Your will be done."

We can't live our lives based on our emotions because our emotions are going to fluctuate.

Discerning God's Voice

How do you know when someone knows the Voice of God or is speaking the mind of God? Well, the first thing that will happen is the information will always line up with the written Word of God. Anytime someone asks you to do something that is in opposition to the Bible, you know it isn't God. If somebody is trying to tell you to do something that God has already revealed in the Word of God is wrong, you need to make a decision that you are not going to do it. Read the Book and find out what God has already said about what they are saying God told them. You need to come to a point where you know the Word and you know the voice of Almighty God for yourself.

How else do you know? You know because God generally speaks to you and is already dealing with you about whatever someone else tells you. Don't just let somebody come and tell you something crazy that God hasn't even told you or spoken to you or isn't dealing with you about. Most of the time what God does when He sends a prophet it is to confirm something He has already dealt with you about.

There are some people who have gotten themselves into trouble because they let somebody with a controlling Jezebel spirit speak things into their lives that did not come from God. You need to come to a point when you understand your relationship with God and when He speaks to you before He speaks through somebody else. He's going to deal with you first.

You need to have a relationship with God and come to a point where you know the voice of your Heavenly Father. You need to come into a relationship with Him so that when He speaks to you, you don't have to check with anybody. When God speaks to you and tells you to do something, you need to know your God intimately enough that you can confidently do what He tells you to do.

My sheep heareth My Voice, and they know My Voice, and they follow me. (John 10:27)

How else do you know the Voice of God? You have got to spend time with God. The reason you automatically know if it is or isn't God is because you know that there are certain things that don't sound like Him. For example, I know my wife. If someone came to me and said that she did certain things I'd be able to tell right away if they were telling the truth or not because I have been in her company, I have spent time with her, and I have a relationship with her.

You need to know your God intimately enough that you can confidently do what He tells you to do.

You've got to know your God intimately enough that you know when somebody is a person that represents Him and has heard from Him. That's the kind of relationship that Samuel had with God. When God told him to go to the house of Jesse, he heard God's voice and did what God told him to do. If you are going to let somebody lay their hands upon you, know that this is a person who hears from God.

Key Points:

Know God intimately enough you can confidently do what He tells you to do.

We all need somebody to encourage us and somebody to discourage us.

We all need somebody to be for us and somebody to be against us.

We all need someone to lift us up and someone to down us.

We cannot live our lives based upon our emotions.

It's not over until God says it's over!

God will give you the plan!

Ask Yourself:

Do I know the Voice of God?

Do I need someone else to confirm what I have heard from God?

Do I really know His voice so well I will willingly obey?

Does the person I seek to anoint and lay hands on me know God's voice?

Does what this person is telling me line up with the written Word of God?

Declare:

I want to know my God intimately enough that I can hear His voice and confidently do what He tells me to do. I want the LORD to be with me like He was with Samuel. I want others to know I am established as a servant of the Lord.

CHAPTER 8

Somebody Who Walks in Integrity

The second thing you want to look for is somebody who has and walks in integrity. It is obvious by just a glance at the headlines that we are experiencing a crisis of integrity in our world today. What is integrity? According to the Word of God the Hebrew word is *tôm* which means to be complete or finished with nothing else expected or intended. So in other words, you want to have somebody lay hands on you who is complete, not perfect for you know that would eliminate everybody. It has been said that integrity is what you have left when you have lost everything.

Integrity is what you have left when you have lost everything.

Job was a man of integrity because after he had lost his children, his money, his reputation, and his health he still had his integrity (Job 2:3, 27:5). I wonder how many of us would have anything left if we lost our money, our family, our health, and our reputation. The person that lays hands on you should be someone who walks in completeness. In other words, you don't want anybody laying hands on you who has obvious missing parts, who has gaping holes in their life. You want a person of integrity!

Colossians 2:10 says, "You are complete in Him who is the head of all principality and power" (NKJV). This is the kind of person who has such a relationship with God that they understand that Christ alone makes them complete. I don't need anybody's acceptance to make me feel whole. I don't need you to like me! If you like me, thank God. But if you don't like me it's alright because I'm complete in Him! I don't need to fit in everywhere because I am so complete that I understand that there are some places that I do not belong. I don't have to compromise who I am to be accepted by anybody because I am complete in Jesus.

If you take away my house that's alright, I'm still complete. If you take away my car, I'm still complete. If you take away my clothes, if you walk out on me, I'm still complete in Jesus. If you're going to have someone lay their hands on you make sure that they are complete. Make sure it's somebody who walks in integrity. That's the thing about Samuel. God knew He could trust him. Samuel walked in integrity; his "Yea" was "Yea" and his "Nay" was "Nay." There weren't any grey areas. You were either right or you were wrong. Regardless of what the consequences could be, Samuel was a man who would stand up and tell you the truth. God is looking for somebody who is going to walk in this thing called "integrity."

Truth Protects Integrity

Truth was a part of him and it was that which made Samuel complete. Regardless of what was going on around him he could not depart from the **Truth!** When Samuel was growing up he was living in a time when the priesthood was corrupt, and even as a child he had to make some decisions. He could join in with the sons of Eli who the Bible says were sleeping with the women who came to the outside of the temple and stealing the offerings that were offered unto God (1 Samuel 2:12-

17). He had an opportunity to be in the house and join in with the corruption that was going on.

We all have opportunities to compromise our integrity. People will come and say, "Look, it's okay to do this because everybody is doing it. God understands. He'll just wink at you. No one is going to find out." It is not okay; it is blatant disobedience. Don't listen to somebody who is telling us to do things that are in opposition to the Word of God. It's not okay to hold unforgiveness and walk in anger and in bitterness and don't let anyone, no matter who they are tell you it is.

Samuel had that opportunity. He could have decided that because Eli's sons were doing it that he could just join in and be just like them. God is looking for people with integrity. A lot of people are more like Jello. Jello will fit into whatever the mold is. If you put it in a square mold, it's going to be square. If you put it in a round mold, it's going to come out round. There are too many people whom God cannot depend upon because they just try to fit into the mold of their surroundings.

If people are acting one way and you cannot stand up for right, you're just going to fit into that mold. Not only are you going to start fitting in, if you are with the gossips you'll start gossiping. If you get with the fornicators, you'll start fornicating. If you get with the adulterers, you'll start committing adultery. You just fit in right where you are and have sold out to their influence, mind-set, and your circumstances.

God is looking for somebody who is sold out for Him. I am sold out for Jesus. I will not compromise who I am. I will not lose my completeness. I will not bend or bow and try to fit in to what you want me to be. You can wave the carrot before me and try to tell me that if I change you will do this and do that, but the devil is a liar. If I stand for God, He will promote me in due time. If I humble myself before the hand of Almighty God, He is going to exalt me in due time. I refuse to lose my integrity!

God is looking for somebody who is sold out for Him.

Integrity in Action

That's what I like about Samuel. Samuel's life was integrity in action. When he went before Israel he rebuked them (1 Samuel 7). When they were out of line he told them the truth. When they wanted a king as opposed to following God he became angry and rebuked them for their actions and told them they were on the wrong path (1 Samuel 8). When Saul lied about his disobedience Samuel stood before this king and said, "Listen, here, I've got to speak with integrity." Samuel told Saul that God was going to take the kingdom from him (1 Samuel 13:13-14). When God told Samuel to go to Jesse's house and anoint David, he did what God told him to do.

If you're going to have somebody lay hands on you make sure you have someone who walks in integrity and walks in completeness. I don't want a half-saved person or a half-sanctified individual laying hands on me. I don't want anybody who is half here and half there laying hands on me. I don't want somebody who has joy and peace half the time laying their hands on me. I don't want anybody who's nice half of the time and mean the other half of the time laying their hands on me. I need somebody who is whole, somebody who walks in integrity to lay hands on me, anoint me, and prophecy over me. That's what you need, too.

Never attach yourself to somebody who does not have the integrity to see you go further than they have gone. You need somebody that wants to see God open up more doors for you than they have had the opportunity to walk through themselves. That was the thing about Samuel. Samuel was told to anoint a new king. Up to this time, Samuel had been the judge. Everything was going alright for Israel because they were under the **Voice of God.** God would speak to the Judge, the Prophet Samuel, and Israel would do what the man of God told them to do. But then they wanted a king. Samuel's integrity showed through as he obeyed God in spite of his circumstances and what that obedience would mean to him personally.

But the people refused to listen to Samuel. "No!" they said. "We want a king over us. Then we will be like all the other nations, with a king to lead us and to go out before us and fight our battles." When Samuel heard all that, the people said, he repeated it before the Lord. (1 Samuel 8:19-21 NIV)

Now the day before Saul came, the Lord had revealed this to Samuel: "About this time tomorrow I will send you a man from the land of Benjamin. Anoint him ruler over my people Israel; he will deliver them from the hand of the Philistines. I have looked on my people, for their cry has reached me." When Samuel caught sight of Saul, the Lord said to him, "This is the man I spoke to you about; he will govern my people." (1 Samuel 9:15-17 NIV)

Then Samuel took a flask of oil and poured it on his head, and kissed him and said: "Is it not because the LORD has anointed you commander over His inheritance?" (1 Samuel 10:1 NKJV)

Note: Following 1 Samuel 10:1 in the Masoretic Text, Targum, and Vulgate, the Septuagint reads, "His people Israel; and you shall rule the people of the Lord" and the Septuagint and Vulgate add, "And you shall deliver His people from the hands of their enemies all around them. And this shall be a sign to you, that God has anointed you to be a prince."

After Saul messes up, God tells Samuel to go and anoint another king. He could have had the mind-set, "Hey, why can't I be king? After all, they have been listening to me all this time." The heart of Samuel was such that he made a decision based on integrity, not self-interest. Even though he knew David was going to go higher than he had ever gone, Samuel made up his mind that he was going to be obedient to God. He did not mind seeing David go further than he ever had. When they called this young man into the room that did not have any of the things that said he was great, Samuel heard the voice of God and obeyed Him in spite of what he saw and what it would mean to him personally.

You need to have somebody who's going to speak a word of destiny into your spirit.

That's the kind of person you need to look for when you look for somebody to lay hands on you. You need somebody who is not going to see you where you are but where you are going. You need to have somebody who's going to speak a word of destiny into your spirit. The Bible says that Samuel anointed David with oil, laid his hands upon him and "The Spirit of the Lord rested upon him from that day forward" (1 Samuel 16:13). You need to find somebody that believes in you, somebody that's going to see you rising to great heights, and who recognizes that there is an anointing upon your life.

Not only did Samuel walk in integrity, he passed this principle on to David. When Samuel anointed David and laid hands on him, the spirit of Samuel was also passed on to young David. Psalm 78:72 says, "And

David shepherded them with integrity of heart; with skillful hands he led them" (NIV). Later God told David's son Solomon, "As for you, if you walk before me in integrity of heart and uprightness, as David your father did, and do all I command and observe my decrees and laws, I will establish your royal throne over Israel forever, as I promised David your father" (1 Kings 9:4-5 NIV).

We all need a Samuel in our lives, and we need to become a Samuel in another's life! Then we will truly rule and reign as leaders in the Kingdom of God!

Key Points:

We need someone with integrity to speak a word of destiny into our spirit.

Integrity is what we have left when we have lost everything.

God is looking for somebody who is sold out for Him.

We need a Samuel and need to become a Samuel.

We must not compromise our integrity.

Do not lose your completeness!

We are not made of Jello!

Guard integrity!

Seek Truth!

Ask Yourself:

Am I complete in Him?

Do I need other's acceptance to make me feel whole?

Do I need others to like me in order to feel complete?

Am I willing to compromise when others are doing certain things?

Do I try to fit in to what others want me to do or be?

Am I truly sold out for Jesus?

Do I diligently seek the truth?

Declare:

If I stand for God, He will promote me in due time. If I humble my-self before the hand of Almighty God, He is going to exalt me in due time. I refuse to lose my integrity! I will not compromise who I am! I will not lose my completeness! I will not bend or bow and try to fit in to what others want me to be! I will seek the truth! I am sold out for Jesus!

SECTION FOUR

Eliab

How do you handle it when you are at war with someone who does not like your success?

The Playa Hater

And Eliab his eldest brother heard when he spake unto the men; and Eliab's anger was kindled against David, and he said, why camest thou down hither? and with whom hast thou left those few sheep in the wilderness? I know thy pride, and the naughtiness of thine heart; for thou art come down that thou mightest see the battle. And David said, what have I now done? Is there not a cause? (1 Samuel 17:28-29)

One of the most profound effects of street culture has been its ability to create its own language. This language has been able to transcend into the mainstream of society and literally transform the meaning and use of certain words and phrases. Although it may be more prevalent in our day in which street slang is used on television, especially in the reporting of sporting news, we can actually follow this trend by travelling all the way back to the fifties. This is when the word "cool" became a way to describe one's image. In the seventies when they said someone was wearing a "bad suit," driving a "bad car" or was a "bad brother " or a "bad sister," it became a good thing. Our modern-day slang, "chilling" has nothing to do with feeling cold. A skinny girl can be called fat (phat), and events can be "slamming" though it does not mean that somebody picked it up and threw it on the ground. A jacket can be "dope" and it doesn't mean that you can get high off it, and a CD can be hot yet be able to be touched without the use of oven mitts.

These are just a handful of words that street culture and particularly persons of color have transformed and re-defined and are now used in a totally different manner. These words or phrases are being used in the bedroom, the classroom, and even in the boardroom. They have been taken out of the hand of Webster and the language laws and their use and meaning have been strangely and wonderfully transformed. One of these phrases or words actually finds itself in the title of this chapter: "Playa Hater." Playa (player) does not mean a performer in a drama or one who plays a musical instrument. On the street "playa" can be used to mean a female or male who has a lot of men or a lot of women. Don't be that type of playa.

I also found out that this word can mean someone who is good at what they do, someone who has skills. Therefore, the title of this chapter, "Playa Hater" is someone who hates someone or is jealous of someone simply because they have skills and have used them to attain a place of recognition. They are, for one reason or another, angry at someone else's success. They are jealous of someone else's achievements, will not speak to that person, refuses to celebrate their success, and will not participate in a relationship with that person. Therefore, they fall into the category of being a "Playa Hater."

If you are going to do anything significant and really be blessed in your life, you've got to make up your mind and come to the realization that you are going to have to deal with "playa haters." If you are successful, you are going to have to deal with some insecure people who have inferiority complexes that will not like you simply because you are better at what you do than they are. They will hate you because you have an anointing on your life and that someone is celebrating you instead of them. Let me warn you as somebody who has lived through it before. Watch out for the playa hater!

What you have to do is be wise enough to keep one eye on God and one eye on the Playa Hater.

Watch Out for the Playa Haters

Playa Haters will assassinate you if they can. They will plot against you and try everything they can to try to stomp out your vision and remove you from the place in which God has destined for you. They will smile in your face, but they are back-stabbers who want to take your place. You need to understand that there are people who are filled with jealousy and envy, and you've got to deal with them wisely and keep your focus upon God. They might be the person who brought you to church in the first place. They may be the person in the cubicle next to you on your job. They may sit on your Board, sing in your choir, sit next to you in church or be an artificial friend. What you have to do is be wise enough to keep one eye on God and one eye on them. Some folks will hate you based upon your success.

Don't hate the playa, hate the game!

The thing that makes dealing with playa haters so difficult is the source from which they come. You see, we would be better prepared to deal with playa haters if somehow, they came dressed in the outfit of the enemy. If they were wearing war garments that were clearly marked with the insignia of the demoniac or if they were clearly outside the church and out in the world, we could understand them and know where they are coming from. The thing about playa haters, however, is that many times they exist and mount their attack right in the midst of our family. That is what made David's battle so difficult. The playa hater in his life was actually his very own brother, Eliab.

When you look through the Word you see other brothers that were playa haters. It was a brother named Cain who murdered Abel out of jealousy. It was a conniving brother, by the name of Jacob, who stole Esau's birthright. It was his brothers who sold Joseph into slavery. It was a brother who did not welcome the Prodigal Son back home. It is difficult when you find that the person in your life who is supposed to be supporting and standing by you is filled with envy, jealousy, and wanting to take you out. It is difficult to deal with playa haters when they are your brothers and sisters in your natural family or in the family of God.

Eliab was actually the oldest of David's seven brothers. He shows up about ten times within the pages of Scripture, but there are two very significance times when Eliab had a profound impact on the life of David. His first appearance is at the anointing service for David in which it was revealed that David would be the next king over Israel. One chapter later when David is sent out by Jesse to take lunch to his brothers who were serving in Israel's military, we find Eliab showing up one more time. When David arrives to deliver the meal, the Israelites are being challenged by a giant by the name of Goliath. Eliab's presence and David response in both of these scenes tell us something about the mindset of playa haters as well as how we are supposed to deal with them.

CHAPTER 9

Eliab's Frustrations

As we study the Scriptures, they will teach us a godly response to Eliab, the Playa Hater. If you are going to have victory and respond correctly, the first thing you have to do is to try to understand his frustration. If the truth were known, Eliab really does not hate you, he actually hates himself. He hates himself in the sense that he has not developed in himself the eternal things that are invisible that makes life worthwhile and results in capturing the favor of God.

I have often been asked, "How do I deal with difficult people in the church? What is it that has enabled me to maintain my cool and not explode and respond to them in the wrong manner?" I've learned what you have to do is try to understand why they act like they do. The Christian psychologist, Clyde Narramore, simply says, "Problems seldom stand alone." What that means is that many times when you see a person's behavior, there are usually things that are driving them to make them act like they act. If you get close enough to look into their life and their psyche, you will find that there are a myriad of issues that motivate their deviant and destructive behavior.

Don't take this statement as an excuse to let crazy people stay in your life, ruin your life, and mess you up. Use it to help you understand why they behave like they behave. Many times, that person is looking for love and acceptance. Many times, that person is behaving like they are because they're masking their own insecurity. Many times, they are using defense mechanisms to protect themselves from further hurt.

They are dissatisfied and miserable. We know that misery likes company so that they will try to make you miserable also. They suffer in their own lives from the pain of blown opportunities. In other words, people don't always act crazy, mean, and wicked just to act crazy, mean, and wicked. Many times, there are things that are driving them. If we can help them to understand themselves, it will help us to respond in a way that won't lower us to their level and help them in the process. That's why you've got to get an understanding of what is driving this playa hater.

Beware the Superiority Complex

When they had come, he looked on Eliab [the eldest son] and said, Surely the Lord's anointed is before Him. But the Lord said to Samuel, Look not on his appearance or at the height of his stature, for I have rejected him. For the Lord sees not as man sees; for man looks on the outward appearance, but the Lord looks on the heart. (1 Samuel 16: 6-7 AMP)

The problem with playa-hating people like Eliab is that they are frustrated with their own lives. Eliab and David had grown up in the same house. They had all the same opportunities. In fact, Eliab had more opportunities than David. They went to the same schools, the same prayer meetings, had the same teachings, and the same Bible studies. All of these things were the same except Eliab was in a greater position than David because he was the eldest son. During this era in Jewish history, the firstborn in every home was the privileged child. Eliab had all the advantages. He was the one who was going to get most of the inheritance if his daddy were to die. He was the one who was going to have all of the opportunities.

Here was a boy who was in a privileged position, but his privileges ended up ruining his thought process. He figured that he was in; he'd made it and did not have to do all of that sheep-watching stuff that David was doing. He developed a superiority complex and said, "My position is solidified as long as I look the part, wear all the right clothes, show up every now and then, and know all the rules." He had pull. He had position. He had connections. He had all of the exterior things that looked like he could be the chosen one.

While Eliab was basking in the life of the firstborn son, David was out in the field watching the sheep, being faithful, and submitting to his father. He was out there writing and worshipping. He was out there learning how to enjoy the presence of God, learning about the love of God, learning about the power of God, and learning about the anointing that had been placed upon his life.

I believe that every now and then Eliab looked out the window and saw crazy David out there dancing and shouting among the sheep. He may have sneered every now and then at David and thought to himself that David would never amount to anything. The difference was that while David was having church, Eliab was playing church. God knows the difference. He knows the motivation of the heart. He knows our attitude and our mind-sets. Eliab may have had everybody fooled, but God cannot be fooled.

Eliab had all of the exterior things going for him, but the problem was that when God started looking for a king He measured by a different standard. The things that Eliab needed were not on his résumé. God did not come looking for brains, beauty, and body. Neither did he come looking for lips, hips, and fingertips. He didn't come looking for the size of somebody's house or the size of their bank account. He was looking for somebody whose heart was right with God. Eliab had spent all of his life investing in all of the wrong things.

Eliab had the look, the position, and the wealth. The problem is God is not impressed by our looks. God is not impressed by our house, our position or our money. God is looking for somebody who has a heart that is right with Him. God wants to know how this person worships Him. He wants to know how they treat God's people. Do they have the kind of love that is needed for such a time as this? What are the motivations of their heart? That's what God is looking for. When Eliab stepped up to the plate and thought that they probably were going to anoint him, God said, "Samuel, I don't even want you looking at his outward appearance for I do not look at his outward appearance. I am looking upon the man's heart." God is looking for somebody who has a heart that will respond to Him. That's why God chose David instead of Eliab.

God is looking for somebody who has a heart that will respond to Him.

It is always frustrating when you work on the things that you thought were getting favor with God only to find out that they were all the wrong things. You reach a point where your connections run out. Your company goes belly up. You lose your coke bottle figure. When these kinds of people realize all the things they thought were going to get them somewhere have failed, instead of getting it right, they start mistreating people and try to make people feel as frustrated as they are. Since they can't have it, they certainly won't let you have it. They'll do everything to make people feel inferior to them. They'll even try to usurp the anointed, chosen one. They will anoint and appoint them-selves and then bully their way to success and respect. People like Eliab will do everything they can do to stop the chosen, anointed one like Da-vid from getting there.

God's Divine Reversal

In these last days, God is doing what I like to call a "Divine Rever-sal." Anyone who thinks they have the qualifications and think they're so superior, God is pulling them down. He is raising up people who are like David, who have a heart after Him. They may not have a lot of money, but they have a heart after Him. They may not have all the skills and education, but they have a heart after Him. The first shall become last and the last are becoming first. He's making the top the bottom and the bottom the top. The rich are becoming poor and the poor are be-coming rich. Servants are becoming kings and kings are becoming serv-ants! Get ready! God is reversing this thing! I don't know about you, but I want my heart at a place where I can say "Yes" to the will of Almighty God and be ready for what God is about to do!

Jesus replied, "This is the Great Reversal: many of the first ending up last, and the last first." (Matthew 19:30 MSG)

But many who [now] are first will be last [then], and many who [now] are last will be first [then]. (Matthew 19:30 AMP)

I can see Eliab walking into that room thinking that he had it all together, "I'm surely the man." But God spoke to the prophet and said, "Don't consider his height for I have rejected him." Then Samuel spoke and said to Jesse, "Are these all your sons?" He said, "No I've got one more but he's out there watching the sheep. He has no qualifications.

He's not like Eliab." But the prophet said, "Bring him in here for we will not sit down until he comes." When David came into the room Samuel anointed him with oil symbolizing that God's Spirit was upon him preparing him to be the next king.

If your heart is right before God, God's got an anointing He wants to place upon you.

David and Eliab both attended the same service. David left anointed but Eliab left frustrated. Isn't it something when you can attend the same service and hear the same Word, but one person's heart is right and the other person's heart is full of envy and jealousy? David leaves anointed and the playa hater leaves with an attitude.

Don't be on the playa hater side of the game. Don't get mad because God blesses another. Don't get frustrated because another receives a Word from God. Get your heart right with God and you'll be the David not the Eliab.

Key Points:

God is looking for somebody who has a heart that will respond to Him.

The Great Reversal is the first end up last and the last end up first.

God's anointing is only for those with a heart right with Him.

A heart right with God produces a David not an Eliab.

Eliab fooled others, but God cannot be fooled.

Keep one eye on God, one eye on Eliab.

Beware the Superiority Complex!

Beware the Playa Hater!

Be David no Eliab!

Ask Yourself:

Do I truly worship God?

How do I treat God's people?

Do I have the kind of love that is needed for such a time as this?

What are the motivations of my heart?

Have I been on the playa hater side of the game?

Do I get mad because God blesses another?

Do I get frustrated because another receives a Word from God?

What do I need to do to get my heart right with God?

Declare:

I will not be found on the playa hater side of the game. I will do what it takes to get my heart right before God so I can receive the anointing He wants to place upon me. I will not get frustrated when others are blessed, I will rejoice with them. I will serve where God calls me to serve and follow the path, He has chosen for me no matter what I see Him doing in other people's lives.

CHAPTER 10

Ignore Eliab's Evaluations and Focus on Your Own Assignment

A fool finds no pleasure in understanding but delights in airing his own opinions. (Proverbs 18:2 NIV)

Not only must we understand this playa hater's frustration, but we must learn to ignore his evaluation and not lose our focus. The thing about playa haters is that somehow, they feel that they are anointed to evaluate our performance and our worth. The problem is they are not qualified, and they do it from a skewed and selfish standard. Therefore, if we are not doing it how they would do it or how they want us to do it, they will try to give us a negative evaluation. We must be open to constructive criticism, but we do not have to listen to everybody's evaluation or opinion. As a matter of fact, the quickest way to insanity is to try to live your life based on the opinion of others.

Webster defines the word opinion as "absolute certainty or positive knowledge; not what seems true, valid or probable to one's own mind." A person's opinion has nothing to do with fact. It's just what they think about the way things should be. I got to thinking what would happen if I tried to pastor based on everyone's opinions. Some believe that a pastor should be serious all of the time. Some think he should be comical all the time. Some think he should drive a big car. Some think he should drive a small car. Some think he should be frugal. Some think he should be stand-offish. Some think he should shake everybody's hands. Some think he should go out the back door after the service, get in his car, and drive home. Some think he should hang out with this group or that group. Some think he should be poor, and some think he should be rich.

I have discovered that God can tell the pastor things that He has not begun to speak to anyone else about. The pastor cannot live his life based upon the opinions and evaluations of people. We all need to learn how to ignore certain evaluations, or they may keep us from fulfilling what God has called us to do.

David's Transition

David was the youngest. And the three oldest followed Saul. But David occasionally went and returned from Saul to feed his father's sheep at Bethlehem. Then Jesse said to his son David, "hen Jesse said to his son Davidephhah of this dried grain and these ten loaves, and run to your brothers at the camp. And carry these ten cheeses to the captain of their thousand, and see how your brothers fare, and bring back news of them. Now Saul and they and all the men of Israel were in the Valley of Elah, fighting with the Philistines. So David rose early in the morning, left the sheep with a keeper, and took the things and went as Jesse had commanded him. And he came to the camp as the army was going out to the fight and shouting for the battle. For Israel and the Philistines had drawn up in battle array, army against army. And David left his supplies in the hand of the supply keeper, ran to the army, and came and greeted his brothers. (1 Samuel 17:14-15, 17-22 NKJV)

Here is the point where David begins to transition. Up to this point, David has been a shepherd boy doing what his father told him to do.

Once again, he steps out on a journey being committed as a servant. When he left his father's house and headed for the Valley of Elah, he did not know that God was transitioning him. When he reaches to the camp, the troops were scared because Goliath was walking out in the valley and defying the armies of Israel. According to the Word of God this giant was approximately ten feet tall.

Then as he talked with them, there was the champion, the Philistine of Gath, Goliath by name, coming up from the armies of the Philistines; and he spoke according to the same words. So, David heard them. And all the men of Israel, when they saw the man, fled from him and were dreadfully afraid. So, the men of Israel said, "Have you seen this man who has come up? Surely he has come up to defy Israel; and it shall be that the man who kills him the king will enrich with great riches, will give him his daughter, and give his father's house exemption from taxes in Israel."

Then David spoke to the men who stood by him, saying, "What shall be done for the man who kills this Philistine and takes away the reproach from Israel? For who is this uncircumcised Philistine, that he should defy the armies of the living God?"

And the people answered him in this manner, saying, "So shall it be done for the man who kills him."

Now Eliab his oldest brother heard when he spoke to the men; and Eliab's anger was aroused against David, and he said, "Why did you come down here? And with whom have you left those few sheep in the wilderness? I know your pride and the insolence of your heart, for you have come down to see the battle."

And David said, "What have I done now? Is there not a cause?"

(1 Samuel 17:23-29 NKJV)

Eliab heard David talking with the soldiers and burned with anger at him. Notice that as long as David was in the field, Eliab was not bothering him. But now that he is transitioning to another level, Eliab has a problem. The Bible says that Eliab spoke up and began to evaluate David. He asked David why he had come down there because he was supposed to be out there in the field with the sheep not there with the soldiers on the battlefield. He tried to put David in the place where he thought David belonged. Eliab did not know that David did not belong out there in the sheepfold anymore. That was then but this is now! Then Eliab started to evaluate him, "I know how conceited you are and how wicked your heart is. You've come down here only to watch the battle."

I can only imagine what David might have between thinking right then. "Alright, you think that I should be looking after the sheep and you're talking about my heart. You don't remember the service we had at our daddy's house when you walked in to get anointed before me and because of your heart problem God chose me instead of you. Now you've got the nerve to stand here and accuse my heart of being wicked? You forgot about that, didn't you? You can hate me all you want and evaluate me all you want, but I know what God has for me is going to take me to the next level." He literally had to reject the evaluation of his brother in his mind, but not react to it in a way that would not be pleasing to the Lord.

Maybe there is someone in your life who is telling you that you are not going to amount to anything, that you'll never go anywhere, and that you'll never have what God has for you. You need to stop listening to their evaluation. They are jealous and envious. You need to remember the day that God anointed you and chose you for such a time as this. You need to stop listening to everybody's evaluation of you, ignore them, and begin to focus on your own assignment.

Never allow playa haters to cause you to lose focus as to what God has called you to do.

Focus On Your Assignment

Never allow playa haters to cause you to lose focus as to what God has called you to do. Stay focused. One of the goals of playa haters is to try to get you to lose your focus and turn it back on them. If you are taking the time to fight them and answer them back, then they've partly won the battle. When people are evaluating you, you have to only focus in on what God has for you.

Eliab accused David of just coming to sit on the sidelines and watch the battle. What he did not know was that David did not come to see the battle, he came to get involved in the battle. Eliab's problem was that he was all talk. He was authorized to fight Goliath but was afraid to go into battle against the giant. He was already in the military and could have stepped in and said, "I'll do it!" He was afraid. Now that David stepped up to do it, Eliab got an attitude. He'd rather not see it get done than see somebody else do it. So he is trying to evaluate David to get his focus off what David knows he is supposed to do.

He then turned away to someone else and brought up the same matter, and the men answered him as before. What David said was overheard and reported to Saul, and Saul sent for him. (1 Samuel 17:30-31 NIV)

David did not stand there and argue with his brother. He turned from him to talk to another soldier. He did not waste time arguing with someone who could not help him achieve his goal, he focused on his assignment. He turned from the negative people to someone who was positive. He turned from somebody who was discouraging to someone who would encourage him. He turned from somebody who was not a worshipper to somebody who was a worshipper. He turned from someone who was a playa hater to someone who would participate and would celebrate with him.

God will prepare a table for us right in the presence of our enemies.
Many times we get discouraged because we step out to do something for God and people start hating and evaluating us. We want to give up and walk away. Regardless of what somebody has to say, regardless of their criticism, God has called you and me to be giant killers. Playa haters will keep talking but do not listen to them. God has called us to slay the giant, and if God is for you and God is for me, who can be against us. God has raised us up for such a time as this. Let them hate, let them criticize but God will prepare a table for us right in the presence of our enemies. There is a blessing that God has for us even in the midst of our Eliab, our playa-hater!

Key Points:

God has a blessing for us even in the midst of our Eliab, our playa hater.

God prepares a table for us right in the presence of our enemies.

We must be open to constructive criticism but not opinions.

We can't let playa haters cause us to lose our focus.

We must stop listening to their evaluations.

The Lord is to be our Shepherd.

He will lead and guide us.

We have the victory!

God's team wins!

Always!

Ask Yourself:

Have I been listening to negative evaluations from playa haters?

Have I allowed the criticism of others to take my focus off what God has called me to do?

Have I engaged in small and meaningless arguments that have distracted me?

Am I open to constructive criticism?

Have I been overly influenced by the opinions of others?

Declare:

I don't have time to be dealing with small answers, small issues, and small questions. I'm getting my focus back. God has anointed me and He has called me for such a time as this. I don't have time to sit here and let anyone evaluate and criticize me. I see my battle is in front of me and God is going to give me the victory.

SECTION FIVE
Goliath

We all have a giant! That inner or even outer struggle that threatens to ruin us, and that possesses the latent ability to destroy everything that we have labored to build and to obtain in our lives.

The Giant Who Can Make or Break Me

Now the Philistines gathered together their armies to battle, and were gathered together at Shochoh, which belongeth to Judah, and pitched between Shochoh and Azekah, in Ephesdammim. And Saul and the men of Israel were gathered together, and pitched by the valley of Elah, and set the battle in array against the Philistines.

And the Philistines stood on a mountain on the one side, and Israel stood on a mountain on the other side: and there was a valley between them. And there went out a champion out of the camp of the Philistines, named Goliath, of Gath, whose height was six cubits and a span. And he had an helmet of brass upon his head, and he was armed with a coat of mail; and the weight of the coat was five thousand shekels of brass. And he had greaves of brass upon his legs, and a target of brass between his shoulders. And the staff of his spear was like a weaver's beam; and his spear's head weighed six hundred shekels of iron: and one bearing a shield went before him.

And he stood and cried unto the armies of Israel, and said unto them, Why are ye come out to set your battle in array? Am not I a Philistine, and ye servants to Saul? Choose you a man for you and let him come down to me. If he be able to fight with me, and to kill me, then will we be your servants: but if I prevail against him, and kill him, then shall ye be our servants, and serve us. (1 Samuel 17:1-9)

Whether we will admit it or not there is a negative issue in each of our lives that has the potential to make us or break us. There is something either hidden or exposed that we battle with periodically or even on a day-to-day basis that possesses the latent ability to destroy everything that we have worked and labored to build and to obtain in our lives. There is that inner or even outer struggle that threatens to ruin us. Its presence seems to make just surviving a difficult task to achieve. That thing that can sometimes overwhelm us, that challenges us both day and night, and looms over our lives like a dark storm cloud that wants to rain upon our happiness and rob us of our joy. That something that we can identify as our Giant.

Our giant seems invulnerable and often reminds us of its ferocity and its fierceness. A raging giant raves in the valley of our conscious and subconscious minds, threatening to do irreparable harm to our reputation and to our family. Regardless of how spiritual we may be, we all have either had to face or will have to face our giant. We all have a giant. We may be Saved, sanctified, and filled with a double dose of the Holy

Ghost, but each and every one of us have a giant that we have to face somewhere.

Just in case the enemy has fooled you into thinking that you don't have one, that you are so spiritually deep, that you never had to face it, let me just take a moment and identify some of those giants. Your giant might be that destructive habit that you can't confess or face up to and that keeps you in a vicious cycle of bondage. Your giant might be that haunting secret act of abuse and shame that drags you back and forth between despair and hope and just won't go away. Your giant might be that mountain of financial debt that has you robbing Peter to pay Paul and has American Express calling to tell you to please leave home without it.

Regardless of how spiritual we may be, we all have either had to face or will have to face our giant.

Your giant might be that besetting sin that keeps tripping you up no matter how hard you seem to pray and even fast for deliverance. Your giant can be that diet plan that you keep breaking every other week. It could be the marriage that has gone from wedlock to deadlock, from the ideal to an ordeal that not even Dr. Phil seems to be able to counsel back together. Your giant can be that elusive educational goal that you cannot discipline yourself to go after. Your giant can be that drug habit, that wayward child, that gossiping tongue, that bad attitude or that spirit of procrastination. That's the bad news.

Giants Can Be Conquered!

The good news is that giants are made to be conquered. As a matter of fact, I have found out that giants are actually sent into our lives for a season and they either make us or break us. The God that we serve desires that these giants be used to build us up. The very thing that we fear the most is often the very thing that God would allow to be used to do a new thing in us. Sometimes those giants are sent to increase our faith in both God and ourselves. Sometimes they are sent to help us to make a statement to demonic forces that we are God's children, and he does not rule in our lives anymore. Sometimes they are sent to show everyone else around us what God has put in us. Whether we are victorious or defeated is all up to us. We will either handle our giant or it will handle us. It is either going to defeat and control us or we are going to defeat and control it.

Giants are sent into our lives for a season and either make us or break us.

Somewhere in the course of this life all of us are going to have to deal with our giants. Somewhere we are all going to have to roll up our sleeves and tell Goliath, "I've had enough of your stalking. I've had enough of your threats. From this day forward I am standing up to you and whether I live or whether I die I'm going to deal with this giant."

Interestingly enough, the most famous battle in the pages of Scripture was not fought between two armies or nations, but it was one that was actually fought between two people. One was David and the other was the giant that would walk into his life, catapult him into the limelight, and make his name a household word in the nation of Israel. The giant was Goliath of Gath which actually means "an exile, stout or sorcerer." Goliath was about nine and a half feet tall and believed to be the largest man known in the history of the world. His coat of armor went from shoulder to knee covering and protecting against the enemy's weapons and is believed to have weighed between one hundred and seventy-five to two hundred pounds. His spear was said to weigh between twenty and twenty-five pounds. His shield was the height of an ordinary full-grown man. He also wore a bronze helmet on his head, bronze leggings to cover his shins, and carried a bronze javelin to help him to strike from a distance. In other words, Goliath was armed to the teeth.

Goliath represented the Philistines who had been the archenemy of Israel for many years. He would step out into the valley on a daily basis calling for someone to do battle against him and bringing terror and fear to the people and the men of Israel. The Bible says that no man was willing to take him up on his challenge. That is not until David, who was simply delivering a lunch to his brothers, heard his threats and curses against the God of Israel. We want to take a look at the actions and the mind-set of David as he teaches us how to deal with the giants who have the potential to make or break us.

CHAPTER 11

We Must Be Courageous

For God hath not given us the spirit of fear; but of power, and of love, and of a sound mind. (2 Timothy 1:7)

The first thing David shows us is that we **must be courageous.** One of the tools of warfare that the enemy will use against us is the paralyzing tool of intimidation and fear. Fear is that affliction of the mind that arises with the awareness of approaching danger. A partner of fear is anxiety. Anxiety is different because when we have anxiety, we not only fear what is coming, but we start worrying about what could come and what could happen. Many times, believers find themselves wrapped up in worrying about things that probably will never happen. Fear has a way of producing panic and paralysis. It has a way causing our thought process to be interrupted. Fear is not an emotion that comes from God. The Bible tells us that God has not given us the spirit of fear.

There is no fear in love; but perfect love casteth out fear: because fear hath torment. He that feareth is not made perfect in love. (1 John 4:18)

That word "torment" means "punishment" and "affliction." Understand the enemy uses fear as intimidation. That is one of the tools of witchcraft and is a sign that the spirit of Jezebel is at work. We've got to get enough confidence in God and enough confidence in ourselves, that regardless of whom we're standing in front of, we refuse to be intimidated. Jesus never used the tool of intimidation to get anybody to submit. We've got to come to a point where we refuse to allow that spirit to take over in our life.

The enemy will try to use fear because he understands that fear has a paralyzing effect. A friend once said, "Fear causes people to draw back from situations. It brings on mediocrity. It dulls the senses. It dulls creativity. It sets one up to be a loser in life."

Fear causes people to draw back from situations, brings on mediocrity, dulls the senses and creativity, and sets one up to be a loser in life.

Courage is the opposite of fear. It means to show oneself strong, to be alert, agile, quick, and energetic. Notice that while fear brings paralysis, courage makes us alert, agile, and quick.

In 1 Samuel 17:1-3 it says the Philistines stood on a mountain on one side of a valley and the army of Israel stood on a mountain on the other side. In order to get real victory, someone had to be courageous enough to go down into the valley and confront the giant. Anybody can be courageous when they are on top of the mountain. Anybody can be courageous when they are naming and claiming it. Anybody can be courageous while the blessings of God are flowing.

God is looking for somebody who is courageous enough to say, "I'm going to walk down into that valley and into the dark, low places and deal with my giant. Even if I can't see him, I've got enough confidence in my God that I'm going to have victory. I'm willing to go down into the valley and get my victory."

Notice what Goliath says in 1 Samuel 17:8-9, "And he stood and cried unto the armies of Israel, and said unto them, why are you come out to set your battle in array? Am not I a Philistine, and ye servants to

Saul? Choose you a man for you, and let him come down to me. If he be able to fight with me, and to kill me, then will we be your servants: but if I prevail against him, and kill him, then shall ye be our servants, and serve us."

Whatever you fear you will end up serving. Whenever you fear something, you are making that thing or that person your god. What you are actually saying is this thing or this person is bigger than the God that you serve. But when you're courageous and you have confidence in your God, you know that no weapon that is formed against you shall prosper. You know that regardless of how big it is, nothing is bigger than your God. You don't have to be afraid of anybody. You can walk with confidence knowing that if God be for you no one can stand against you. It might be bigger than you, but it isn't bigger than your God. It may have more muscle than you, but it isn't stronger than your God. David knew and understood this principle.

Then David said to the Philistine, "You come to me with a sword, with a spear, and with a javelin. But **I come to you in the name of the LORD of hosts, the God of the armies of Israel**, whom you have defied. This day **the LORD will deliver you into my hand,** and I will strike you and take your head from you. And this day I will give the carcasses of the camp of the Philistines to the birds of the air and the wild beasts of the earth, that all the earth may know that there is a God in Israel. (1 Samuel 17:45-46 NKJV)

Your Goliath may be able to conquer you if you try to stand all by yourself, but you can refuse to be afraid because you've got God standing by you. One person plus God is a majority. No giant that you are going to have to deal with is bigger than the God whom you serve. Your

God is great! He's an awesome God and He holds the power of the world in His hands.

Notice what the Philistine giant does in verse 16. He drew near morning and evening. He presented himself for forty days. He was not just bringing fear, but he was bringing a haunting consistent terror. That's the goal of terrorism. He stepped out in the morning when the Israelites were about to start their day and then again at the end of the days so it was the last thing they thought about before they went to bed. Terror by day and terror by night! David understood this principle as well. Look at what he wrote in Psalm 91:1-6.

He that dwelleth in the secret place of the Most High shall abide under the shadow of the Almighty. I will say of the Lord, He is my refuge and my fortress: my God; in Him will I trust. Surely, he will deliver thee from the snare of the fowler, and from the noisome pestilence. He shall cover thee with his feathers, and under his wings shall thou trust: his truth shall be thy shield and buckler. **Thou shalt not be afraid for the terror by night; or for the arrow that flieth by day; Nor for the pestilence that walketh in darkness, nor for the destruction that wasteth at noon-day.**

Read these other scriptures on courage and receive the encouragement of the Lord no matter what Goliath you are facing in your life.

Have not I commanded thee? Be strong and of a good courage; Be not afraid, neither be thou dismayed: for the Lord thy God is with thee whithersoever thou goest. (Joshua 1:9)

The Lord is my light and my salvation; whom shall I fear? The Lord is the strength of my life; of whom shall I be afraid? (Psalm 27:1)

Key Points:

Fear brings on mediocrity, dulls the senses, and creativity.

Fear causes people to draw back from situations.

Whatever we fear we will end up serving.

God has not given us the spirit of fear.

Whatever we fear becomes our god.

Courage is the opposite of fear.

One plus God is a majority.

Be courageous!

Ask Yourself:

What is the giant I am facing in my life today?

How am I going to handle my giant?

Do I have confidence that with God I can have the victory?

Am I in the secret place of the Almighty?

Is the Lord the strength of my life?

Of whom am I afraid?

Declare:

I'm going to walk down into that valley and into the dark, low places and deal with my giant. Even if I can't see him, I've got enough confidence in my God that I'm going to have the victory. Even though I'm walking in a dark place and not even able to see my hand in front of me, I have enough courage in my God that I'm willing to go down into the valley and get my victory. I've had enough of your stalking, Goliath. I've had enough of your threats. From this day forward I am standing up to you and whether I live or whether I die I'm going to deal with my giant.

CHAPTER 12

We Must Be Confrontational

Then David spoke to the men who stood by him, saying, God will give you courage. He will give you the victory. If you believe you shall be! So Israel? For who is this uncircumcised Philistine, that he should defy the armies of the living God? (1 Samuel 17:26 NKJV)

We must be *confrontational.* I heard one preacher say, "We cannot conquer what we will not confront." One of the worst places to exist is called "Denial." Often the opposite of confrontation is denial. We try to act like things don't exist. We have learned how to practice denial. It amazes me how we can know that we have a problem, know it is paralyzing or even killing us, and we do nothing about it. The house is on fire, but we act like it is not happening. The problem really is that we love appearance more than reality. As long as things appear that they are alright most of us think that we really are alright.

The problem with denial is that if we don't deal with our issues than our private issue becomes a public issue. The thing that we are wrestling with in private, pretty soon we'll be wrestling with it in the open. Denial is when we hide our heads in the sand like the ostrich and pretend whatever it is has disappeared. The problem does not go away just because we try to ignore it or pretend it isn't there.

Denial is when we hide it, ignore it or pretend it isn't there.

The other problem with denial is that by refusing to confront something by putting our heads in the sand, we often turn our backs on it and leave our backs vulnerable. It reminds me of the show "Sanford and Sons" where Fred Sanford is about to take some karate lessons. He is there with the instructor who is talking about what he's about to get involved with. He tells Fred that this form of Karate is the oldest form of self-defense known to man. Fred Sanford turned to him and said, "It ain't older than running." The oldest self-defense mechanism is running away from confrontation!

When we look at the armor of God, it does not protect our backs. There's a reason for that. God does not want us running from the devil. The Bible says we are to run from youthful lusts. However, when it comes to the devil and the giants in our lives the Bible says, "Resist the devil and he will flee from us" (James 4:7). When we take off running, we actually make ourselves more vulnerable to our giant.

When the men of Israel saw Goliath, they fled. They were running, trying to get away from their giant instead of confronting it. Notice what happens as the men refuse to confront the giant. When Goliath first came out, he said choose a man and let him come down to me. Then the Bible says that the men of Israel were talking and saying, "Have you seen this man that is come up to defy the armies of Israel" (1 Samuel 17:25). They would not confront him and now he is giant getting closer and bolder. The devil is not just going to stay in one place. "If you give the devil an inch, he will take a mile." When we refuse to confront our demons and our giants, they just get bolder and bolder. We've got to decide that we are going to take a stand. James 4:7 in the Amplified Bible says, "Resist the devil [stand firm against him], and he will flee from you."

When David arrived on the scene, the men were running away from the battle lines and he asked, "Hey, what's going on?" The funny thing is the way they described the giant to David would make one think they knew God was on their side, "Have you seen the man who has come to defy the armies of the Living God?" David boldly says, "Where is this uncircumcised Philistine who would dare to defy the armies of the living God?" In other words, "If you are looking for somebody to fight against him than you have found the man. I'm ready to stand up. Enough is enough!"

It's time to stand up! Enough is enough! It's confrontation time!
When I first confronted this giant that was after me, he was all the way in New York, but because I walked in denial, I found that he was waiting at the airport when I left that city. Since I did not deal with him at the airport, now he's knocking at my front door. Tell that giant, I feel the spirit of David rising up in me! It is **Confrontation Time!**

David's Testimony
Then David said to Saul, "Let no man's heart fail because of him; your servant will go and fight with this Philistine." And Saul said to David, "You are not able to go against this Philistine to fight with him; for you are a youth, and he a man of war from his youth." (1 Samuel 17:32-33 NKJV)
The men around him reported what David was saying to King Saul. They said, "There's a boy out there wanting to take on Goliath." Saul sent for him and brought him into his chambers. "Who are you that you would stand up to fight against this giant? I don't see any stripes on you!

I don't see any medals. I don't see your name on the military list. Who do you think you are?"

One of the problems with us when we are facing our giants is too many times we forget what we're supposed to remember and remember what we're supposed to forget. Isn't it funny how we can win ninety-nine times and lose once, but when the devil backs us in a corner all we can focus on is that one defeat. You're trying to get back in school, but you failed one class ten years ago and all the devil has you focusing on is that one failed class. You've got a 4.0 in all the rest of them, but the enemy is got you focusing on the one failed thing.

But David said to Saul, **"Your servant used to keep his father's sheep, and when a lion or a bear came and took a lamb out of the flock, I went out after it and struck it, and delivered the lamb from its mouth; and when it arose against me, I caught it by its beard, and struck and killed it. Your servant has killed both lion and bear; and this uncircumcised Philistine will be like one of them, seeing he has defied the armies of the living God." Moreover David said, "The LORD, who delivered me from the paw of the lion and from the paw of the bear, He will deliver me from the hand of this Philistine."** (1 Samuel 17:34-37 NKJV)

David came back with a testimony of his former confrontations. David said, "The same God that gave me the lion and the bear shall surely give me the uncircumcised Philistine." When we faced that lion and that bear we were just practicing for that giant. We can have the confidence knowing that the same God that gave us the lion and the bear will surely give us that giant. God is going to have some practice runs in the background for us. We just need to keep on practicing!

I remember when I started preaching at Camp Meetings for the Church of God. I was pretty young, and a lot of folks said, "Who does he think he is? Where does he come from?" What they didn't realize was that at my first church when nobody was paying attention, and when all I had were thirty members in a little run-down church building, God had me practicing. I was back there in the background. God was getting me ready.

David knew that if he faced this Goliath, God would take care of the rest.

When Saul heard David testify, he said, "Go, and the Lord be with you." My opinion is King Saul had the wrong attitude. I think deep down inside Saul thought that David was going to get killed. Maybe he even knew Samuel had anointed him as the next king. At any rate, this mighty king let this young lad go out and confront Goliath.

David knew something Saul had forgotten. David knew that God had been preparing him for such a time as this. David knew that if he faced this Goliath, God would take care of the rest. What God did for David He will do for us, too. Our part is to confront that giant. When we do, God will direct the battle and the victory will be ours!

Key Points:

David knew that if he confronted Goliath, God would take care of the rest.

The problem with denial is we expose our backsides to attack.

Running actually makes us more vulnerable to the giant.

We cannot conquer what we will not confront.

We must stand and fight the giant.

It is **Confrontation Time!**

Enough is enough!

Ask Yourself:

Have I been dealing with denial?

Have I been hiding my head in the sand?

Why am I afraid to confront my Goliath?

What former lions and bears should I be remembering that God has helped me overcome?

Declare:

It's time for me to stand up, so in the Name of Jesus, I declare to my Goliath, enough is enough! I feel the spirit of David rising up in me! It is **Confrontation Time!** Devil, I've had it, enough is enough. I'm tired of walking in depression and discouragement, enough is enough! I'm tired of letting the devil steal my joy, and mess up my family, enough is enough!

CHAPTER 13

We Must Be Complete

As the Philistine moved closer to attack him, David ran quickly toward the battle line to meet him. Reaching into his bag and taking out a stone, he slung it and struck the Philistine on the forehead. The stone sank into his forehead, and he fell face down on the ground. So, David triumphed over the Philistine with a sling and a stone; without a sword in his hand, he struck down the Philistine and killed him. David ran and stood over him. He took hold of the Philistine's sword and drew it from the sheath. After he killed him, he cut off his head with the sword. When the Philistines saw that their hero was dead, they turned and ran. *(1 Samuel 17:48-51 NIV)*

Fighting giants and doing battle is not easy so make sure that if you roll up your sleeves and decide to go down in the valley and deal with the giant that you stay long enough to get complete victory. In order to get complete victory, we have to use our own weapons. If ever you decide to go into a valley with somebody else's weapons or somebody else's testimony you may get what looks like a victory but it won't be a real victory. God wants to give you the victory, but He wants you to make use of the weapons that He has specifically given you. Your weapons are able to be used in your battle and are not for others to use.

Then Saul dressed David in his own tunic. He put a coat of armor on him and a bronze helmet on his head. David fastened on his sword over the tunic and tried walking around, because he was not used to them. "I cannot go in these," he said to Saul, "because I am not used to them." So, he took them off. Then he took his staff in his hand, chose five smooth stones from the stream, put them in the pouch of his shepherd's bag and, with his sling in his hand, approached the Philistine. (1 Samuel 17:38-40 NIV)

Saul tried to arm David with his armor. When David put on Saul's armor he could not move like he wanted to move. He could not battle like he wanted to battle. It did not fit him right. David told Saul, "I've got my own weapons that I've been practicing on the lion and the bear. I've got to use what God has given me. I like the weapons that God has given me. I've got to do it like I know how to do it."

Don't let anybody pressure you into fitting into their mold. Don't let anyone pressure you into being something that you are not. God has given you the weapons you need. Your weapons may not appear to be superior but that's alright. If God gave them to you and He placed an anointing upon you, then He can use that little rock and that little sling-shot to take down the giant.

Don't let anyone pressure into being something that you are not!

We used to sing a song in the church that says, "Little is much when God is in it." The Apostle Paul said, "The weapons of our warfare are not carnal, but they are mighty through God to the pulling down of strongholds" (2 Corinthians 10:4). My little rock and my little slingshot may not look like a whole lot, but once the anointing gets upon them, the yoke shall be destroyed. Zechariah said, "It's not by might, nor by power, but it's by My Spirit, saith the Lord of Hosts" (4:6). David knew he could not fight this battle in his own name and in his own authority. He said, "Hey, giant, you are coming at me with a sword, but I come to you in the name of the Lord."

There is a name that is above every giant. There is a name that has the power to defeat every enemy. There is a name that is above cancer. There is a name that is above heart disease. There is a name that is above your situation. There is a name that is above your pain. That is the name of Jesus! In the name of Jesus, we have the victory!

Goliath was laughing at little David and his weapons, but he sure wasn't laughing when that rock hit him in the head.

Complete the Task to Achieve the Victory

Then David put his hand in his bag and took out a stone: and he slung it and struck the Philistine in his forehead, so that the stone sank into his forehead, and he fell on his face to the earth. (1 Samuel 17:49 NKJV)

The Bible says that Goliath fell on his face to the earth, but was he dead? That's where many of us make the mistake, especially when we're in a valley all by ourselves. Our goal oftentimes is just to get out of the battle. What we don't realize is that the valley is designed to give us complete victory. When we're in our valleys and we're so determined to get out, we don't stay long enough for God to give us complete victory. The giant comes, we take out our little stone and we hit him between the eyes. We start dancing and shouting, and we take off and run out of the valley. Then the giant comes to, he gets strong enough to reach up and pull out that little rock, crawls over by the brook, splashes water in his face, starts getting himself together, and then the next thing we know the same giant that we faced last year or last month, is looking us right in the face again. That's why some of us are bound by the same issues year after year and month after month.

There are some things that are called "thorns in the flesh" like Paul had that God said, "I'm not going to remove it from you but I am going to give you the grace to overcome it" (2 Corinthians 12:7). But then there are some giants that simply need to be killed. We need to stop playing games with it and completely kill it! We need to stop letting it exist in our house and kill that thing!

Therefore, David ran and stood over the Philistine, took his sword and drew it out of its sheath and killed him, and cut off his head with it. (1 Samuel 17:51 NKJV)

David handled it. He went up to the giant he had knocked down with the weapons God had given and took the giant's sword and not only killed him with it, he cut off the giant's head with it. Have you ever gotten the victory to a point where the weapon that the devil was going to use against you became your sword of victory? You went through something that was supposed to kill you, but because you were courageous and you confronted it, the thing that was supposed to kill you ended up being your testimony and your weapon. David took the enemy's sword, put his foot on the top of Goliath's chest and said, "I might have to fight against another giant one day, but I'm going to guarantee that it will not be this one." The Bible says that he took the sword and chopped of Goliath's head.

And when the Philistines saw that their champion was dead, they fled. Now the men of Israel and Judah arose, and shouted, and pursued the Philistines as far as the entrance of the valley and to the gates of Ekron. (1 Samuel 17:51-52 NKJV)

We have to stay long enough in the valley to make our battle complete. After David cut off Goliath's head, the army of Israel that was afraid suddenly got bold, ran into the valley, and chased the Philistine army. Whatever the thing that is tormenting and bringing fear into our lives must be confronted with courage and we must achieve the complete victory. We are fighting this battle for ourselves and for those who come after us. Be courageous, confront the giant, and complete the task!

Key Points:

We have to stay long enough in the valley to make our battle complete.

Complete victory comes when we use our God-given weapons.

Be courageous, confront Goliath, and complete the task!

We can't let others pressure us into their mold

Little is much when our God is in it!

We are to be confrontational!

We are to be courageous!

We are to complete it!

We must kill it!

Dead!

Ask Yourself:

Am I trying to fight this giant using someone else's testimony and weapons?

What are the weapons God has given me to confront this giant in my life?

Have I completed the last task God gave me or is that giant still alive?

What do I have to do to make sure this giant is dead, once and for all?

Declare:

It's time for me to stand up in the Name of Jesus. Today is going to be my day of victory in the Name of Jesus! I am going to be courageous, I am going to confront that giant, and I am going to complete the task using the weapons God has given me.

SECTION SIX

Jonathan

One of the consistent images of friendship in the Bible is the knitting together of two souls. In this knitting of two people, the two become companions and privy to one another's innermost thoughts and feelings resulting in intense emotional attachment. The privileges of the biblical soulmate involve intimacy, loyalty, and an emotional attachment.

My Covenant Friend

Then Jonathan and David made a covenant because he loved him as his own soul. (1 Samuel 18:3)

It seems to me that the older I get the harder it has become to make and develop real friendships. When I speak of friendship I am not just talking about the casual, everyday interaction that I have with those around me at superficial levels. I am talking about the development of something that is real, open, and honest. The reasons that I feel it gets more difficult with age is because the older you get your time seems to be so limited and people are less willing to take and make the time to develop lasting friendships.

More importantly, the older you get the more you discover that people seem to possess an ulterior motive in getting to know you. Oftentimes people come with an agenda that is hidden and draped in a deceptive cloak of friendship. They want to know you because of business connections, your position of influence or perceived power. They want to know you because they want insight into your skill level in terms of how you do what you do. There's nothing necessarily wrong with that, but do you really want them as covenantal friends?

Friendship is like money; easier spent than made.

There are those who will befriend you because they have a design in mind as to what you are supposed to do and where you are supposed to go. Then there are people who just want to get close to you to see what they can get from you. That makes it hard to discern between those who come with different motives and those who come for real and genuine friendship. I found out that people are born with the sin curse in them, and that sin curse tends to make us selfish and self-centered. To really develop friendships that are lasting and real, both parties have to be selfless not selfish. Selfishness simply cannot be a part of the equation.

A true friend thinks of you when all the others are thinking of themselves.

Real friendship is more than giving and receiving. Real friendship wants the best for the other person and not just for themselves. Real friendship knows when to draw close and when to give space. A real friend believes in you when you do not believe in yourself. A real friend accepts you with your good and with your bad but will also encourage you to move forward toward improvement. A real friend will joyfully sing with you when you are on the mountain top, and silently walk with you through the valleys of life. A real friend will strengthen you with his prayers, bless you with his love, and encourage you with his hope. I am sure that you'll agree that real friendship is very difficult to find. Friendship is like money, easier spent than made. Friendship can never reach its peak and its apex until it becomes a covenant friendship.

There's no level of friendship that is greater and more pleasing in the sight of God than a covenant friendship. When I speak of covenant friendship, I speak of one that is developed as two people covenant with God and determine to walk in a godly relationship. A godly relationship is recognized as a Kingdom connection that is designed to glorify and honor the king. A covenant friendship is done with the awesome knowledge that God is the unseen guest at every conversation, and the invisible attendee at every meeting and gathering. Covenant friends come together in order to please God as well as to help each other grow in God. These kinds of relationships produce soul ties. They are not soul ties that influence us toward the negative, but to help us walk in God and do better service for the King.

We don't pull each other down. We are not gossiping buddies who have a smear session that does nothing to build us up in our faith. We do not encourage each other to engage in divisive or corrupt behavior that will disrupt the flow of God's blessings in our lives. We do not get together to engage in secret sins. No, we are covenant partners who recognize that God has given us a divine hook-up to enhance and build us to be better kingdom citizens. These types of friendships are the greatest that can ever be experienced because they bring out the best in us.

That's the kind of friendship that God desires for each and every one of us.

As iron sharpens iron so a man sharpens the countenance of his friend. (Proverbs 27:17)

David and Jonathan's Divine Connection

The Bible is full of Covenant Relationships that God used to lift men and women toward their destiny and to experience a higher level of fulfillment. There are none that rival the level of commitment than the friendship between David and his best friend, Jonathan.

It came to pass when David had made an end of speaking unto Saul, that the very soul of Jonathan was **knit with the soul** of David and Jonathan loved him as his own soul. (1 Samuel 18:1 emphasis added)

After David finished talking with Saul, Jonathan became **one in spirit** with David and he loved him as himself. (1 Samuel 18:1 NIV)

A divine covenant and a spiritual connection were born as the very souls of these two young men were knit together. One of the consistent images of friendship in the Bible is the knitting together of two souls. In this knitting of two people, the two became companions of each other's innermost thoughts and feelings resulting in intense emotional attachment. The privileges of the biblical soulmate involve intimacy, loyalty, and a strong emotional attachment. Even at the death of Jonathan, David would say that the love that they shared together was stronger and did more for him than the love that he would have had from any woman. In other words, David was saying that the friendship he had with Jonathan filled an area in his life that not even a relationship with the opposite sex could fill.

CHAPTER 14

Covenant Friends Are Sacrificial

Saul told his son Jonathan and all the attendants to kill David. But Jonathan had taken a great liking to David and warned him, "My father Saul is looking for a chance to kill you. Be on your guard tomorrow morning; go into hiding and stay there. I will go out and stand with my father in the field where you are. I'll speak to him about you and will tell you what I find out."

Jonathan spoke well of David to Saul his father and said to him, "Let not the king do wrong to his servant David; he has not wronged you, and what he has done has benefited you greatly. He took his life in his hands when he killed the Philistine. The LORD won a great victory for all Israel, and you saw it and were glad. Why then would you do wrong to an innocent man like David by killing him for no reason?"

Saul listened to Jonathan and took this oath: As surely as the LORD lives, David will not be put to death." So Jonathan called David and told him the whole conversation. He brought him to Saul, and David was with Saul as before. (1 Samuel 19:1-7 NIV)

When we look at these two individuals, they actually come from two totally different backgrounds. Jonathan grew up in the palace with a silver spoon in his mouth while David grew up spending his time as a country boy with the smell of sheep on him. Jonathan was refined and royal while David spent his life watching the fields and was uncouth, if you will. Jonathan had royal lineage while David was the forgotten son of Jesse. But when they came together none of that mattered at all because God was in the connection. When God is in a connection it doesn't make any difference where the person came from. It does not make any difference how much money they have or do not have. One person can be rich and the other person can be broke, busted, and disgusted. When it is a divine relationship that is ordained of God, God will knit their souls together.

The interesting thing is that these men had something in common. Jonathan's father was so busy being the king that he did not have the kind of relationship with his father that he needed. David's father had rejected him so they both had a void in their lives. When they met the Bible says that their very souls were knit together. Now, there are some characteristics that their wonderful friendship had that I believe that all covenant friendships must have if they are going to be a blessing.

Jonathan is actually one of the most open-hearted and likeable individuals in the Scriptures. He was a daring and successful young officer in Saul's army. He was skilled in archery for which the men of the tribe of Benjamin were known. It was his misfortune to be caught up in a very difficult situation. He was best friends with David, but at the same time he was the oldest son and heir to the throne of King Saul who wanted to kill David. If anything was to happen to King Saul, Crown Prince Jonathan was supposed to be the one who was to take over. But he became friends with David whom God revealed was going to be the next king of Israel. Jonathan's soul was knit together with the man whom God had designed to literally step over him and take a position that was supposed to be his.

Some people are not going to get their breakthrough and blessing until they learn how to worship God for somebody else's blessing. Instead of sitting there having a pity party, they need to learn how to worship God while God is meeting the need for somebody else. Instead of getting an attitude and getting jealous, they need to give Him praise for blessing their brother or sister. God is looking for somebody who loves somebody else just like they love themselves. God is looking for covenant friends.

Real covenant friends are also willing to watch our backs.
Covenant Friends Are Guardians

Real covenant friends are also willing to watch our backs. There is nothing worse than a friend who is there for us in the good times, but as soon as we get into trouble they are gone.

Proverbs 17:17 says, "A friend loves at all times, and a brother is born for adversity."

Real friends are not going to leave you in a time of battle. You need to have somebody that's going to be there when the chips are down and be willing to stand up and even to take a hit for you. Jonathan was that type of friend.

Covenant friends will look out for our destiny.

Jonathan had to have enough love for David to guard his destiny from a father that wanted to take David out. He had to choose between the practical and the spiritual. Jonathan warned David that his father Saul was looking for a chance to kill him. Jonathan was willing to even go to his father on behalf of David to try to run interference for him so that he could guard the very destiny of the person whom God had designed to step over him and take over the throne.

We need somebody who is willing to run interference and speak to our enemies before they try to destroy us. We need to have somebody on the job who is willing to go to the boss and clear up our name before we get in trouble. Jonathan went before Saul in such a manner that Saul actually ended up changing his mind. David was able to come back to the palace because Jonathan was acting as a guardian of his destiny.

Covenant friends will also give us access to places we cannot go ourselves. Covenant friends will look out for our destiny. The covenant that Jonathan and David had was so deep and profound that even after Jonathan died their covenant lasted beyond the grave. That's a covenant friend.

Key Points:

Lasting and real friendships require that both parties are selfless and not selfish.

A covenant friend thinks of us when all others are thinking of themselves.

A covenant friend will run interference and speak to our enemies.

Friendship can be like money, easier spent than made. True covenant friends watch our backs,

Strengthen us with their prayers,

Encourages us with hope,

Bless us with love!

Ask Yourself:

Am I a covenant friend?

Do I have someone whom I am helping in their walk with God?

Do I watch their back and run interference for them?

Am I willing to stand with them in the good and the bad?

Do I have somebody who is my covenant friend?

Declare:

I will be a true covenant friend to _____ and will strengthen _____ with my prayers, bless _____ with my love, and encourage _____ with hope. I will cover _____ back and run interference for them if needed. I will think of _____ needs before my own. I want to be a Jonathan kind of friend to _____ .

CHAPTER 15

Covenant Friends are Real

Jonathan took off the robe that was on him and gave it to David, with his armor, even to his sword and his bow and his belt. (1 Samuel 18:4 NKJV)

Covenant friends are sacrificial, will cover our backs, and promote our destiny. Covenant friends are also real. The older I get the less time I have to spend time with artificial people. I realize that my time is too important to sit around with people who are pretending to be my friend and pretending that they want to see me succeed. I like to spend my time with people who are willing to keep it real. That's the thing about this relationship between Jonathan and David. Jonathan made a covenant with David because he loved him as himself. You know what Jonathan does. The Bible says he took off the robe that he was wearing and gave it to David along with his sword, his bow, and even his belt.

The Robe

The robe with the royal insignia was a statement to David that Jonathan was forfeiting his power in favor of David. It was also a symbol of vulnerability. He didn't care if David saw him as he really was.

When I was pastoring my first church, I invited some members over for some fellowship. One of the people who came called me the next day and said, "Pastor Lee, I'm going to be leaving the church." When I asked this person why they said, "Because I think you need to come higher. All of that laughing and joking around that you do is not necessary." I said, "If you want me speaking in tongues twenty-four hours a day and shouting and screaming Scripture like I do when I'm up in the pulpit, you've come to the wrong church. I invite you to pack up right now and hit the road because that's not the real me! That's me under the anointing and functioning in my role as a pastor!"

We have to get to the point where we have some people around us where can simply take off our royal robe and relax. We don't have to measure what we say. We don't have to worry about being misinterpreted. We don't have to worry about them taking what we say and running to so and so about it. We've got to have somebody who we can be with who we can really just simply be ourselves.

The Sword and the Bow

Notice, Jonathan takes it to another step. Here is what limits most of us from having that type of vulnerability. The Bible says that Jonathan gave David his sword, a weapon that is used when you are up close to your target. You see, Jonathan was a warrior. When it came to fighting, David and Jonathan were two of the best. Then Jonathan gave David his bow. The bow is used from far away. He said, "Listen, I'm not going to try to kill you up close, and I'm not going to get behind your back and try to shoot you from far away."

The Belt

Then Jonathan took off his belt. The belt was the arsenal and held all of his hidden weapons (kind of like Batman when he uses his utility belt). Jonathan said, "Listen, I don't have any hidden weapons either. I'm giving you everything that I am so that we can be comfortable together, so we can chill together. You don't have to worry about me trying to kill you. If somebody stabs you in the back you won't have wonder if it's me because I am your friend. I'm standing beside you. I believe in you, and this is who I am."

Every man and every woman, no matter how anointed you may be, no matter how much money you may have, you need somewhere where you can relax with someone that is not out to get you. You see, that was Samson's problem. As great as he was, he never had a friend, so he ended up in the wrong lap. Some of us don't have any friends and we are looking for love in all the wrong places and so we are ending up in the wrong lap.

Diana Craig said in her statement, "Oh, the comfort of feeling safe with a person having neither to weigh thoughts or measure words but pouring them all out just as they are; chaff and grain together, certain that a faithful hand will take and sift them. Keep that which is worth keeping and with a breath of kindness blow the rest away."

Real friends are real with you, they are open with you, and they accept you. Not only do they accept you, but they are also willing to call you out. A lot of us in the church don't have friends; we have groupies or people who will only say to us what they think we want to hear. They are like the guy on that commercial that when the other guy comes up and says, "What have you got there?" No matter what the person holding the object says, whether it makes sense or not, the guy says, "Brilliant!" That's how some of the "friends" we surround ourselves act. They're not real friends. They're groupies because they're just saying what they think we want to hear.

A real friend will call you out and say, "I love you, but I don't think you should be doing that. I love you but I don't think you should have been saying that. That wasn't right!" A real friend loves you enough to communicate with you when you are going the wrong way.

Faithful are the wounds of a friend: or faithful is the constructive criticism of a friend. But the kisses of an enemy are deceitful. (Proverbs 27:9)

Ointment and perfume rejoice the heart so does the sweetness of a man's friend by hardy counsel. (Proverbs 27:6)

You need to find somebody that is able to call you out. Somebody who isn't afraid to look you right in the eyes and say, "I love you brother but you were wrong. You need to get it together. You're going down the wrong road. You're doing the wrong thing. You're messing up your home." Don't surround yourself with weak, anemic, lying, deceitful, false friends. Surround yourself with somebody who cares about you enough to pull you aside and speak words of correction into your life. It is better to keep a friend from falling than to help him up after he has fallen.

Key Points:
Real friends tell us we're going the wrong way.

Real friends can be real with one another!

Real friends will stand by one another.

Real friends support one another.

Real friends don't lie to us.

Real friends defend us.

Seek a Jonathan!

Be a Jonathan!

Ask Yourself:
Am I a friend that supports?
Am I willing to stand by my friend?
Do I have a friend I can be real with?
Do I have a real friend who loves me enough to tell me when I am going the wrong way?

Declare:
I will be a real friend so that I will have a real friend. I will be that friend that guards my friend's back, runs interference for them, and is willing to stand up for them. I will seek to have a Jonathan friend in my life that I can be real with and trust with my destiny.

CONCLUSION

"All the King's Men: *Book One – Preparing to Reign*" traced David's life from his birth to his defeat of the giant Goliath and his covenant friendship with Jonathan, King Saul's son. We met David's father, Jesse, who not only overlooked his youngest son, but rejected him as even worthy to participate in the special anointing ceremony Samuel was sent to Bethlehem to perform. We also met Samuel, an man of integrity who heard God's voice and not only anointed young David as the next king of Israel, but also imparts his spirit of integrity into this young shepherd boy. David's brother Eliab belittled and rebuked David as he tried to accomplish what God has called him to do. We watched as David defeated the mighty Goliath, served in King Saul's court, and enjoyed a special relationship with his son, Jonathan, the Crown Prince.

All of these people were placed in David's life to help prepare him to reign over God's people as a servant king. David proved himself faithful over the small things and was gradually promoted up through the ranks until he achieved favor with God and man. The people he had around him helped reveal and develop his heart attitude and mind-set. When God looked at him, He said, "This is a man after My own heart!"

Even the negative comments and evaluations of his brothers did not keep David from taking on the giant and completing the mission that transitioned him out of his role as a shepherd boy into the next phase of his training.

You will want to continue your study of "All the King's Men" in *Book Two – Establishing a New Kingdom* where David is literally run out of the palace and runs for his life, pursued by King Saul and his army. David goes from the palace to the wilderness, and on to the cave of Adullam to complete his training for reigning under the guiding hand of Almighty God Himself. God uses many more relationships during this journey to prepare this shepherd boy to reign as Israel's greatest king!

And Samuel said to Saul, Thou hast done foolishly: Thou hast not kept the commandment of the Lord thy God, which he commanded thee: for now would the Lord have established thy kingdom upon Israel forever. But now thy kingdom shall not continue: the Lord hath sought him a man after his own heart, and the Lord hath commanded him to be captain over his people, because thou hast not kept that which the Lord commanded thee. (1 Samuel 13:13-14)

ABOUT THE AUTHOR

REV. WILLIAM A. LEE, JR.

William A. Lee, Jr. is presently serving the Kingdom of God as the Lead Pastor of Victorious Life Church in Conyers, Georgia. He is Chairman of the Church of God Executive Council of 18. He has served as International Revivalist and Urban Ministry Consultant" appointed August 2018. He has served 9 years as Pastor of Daytona Deliverance Church of God in Daytona Beach, Florida appointed August 2009. He served as the State USA Discipleship/Evangelism Director for Florida-Cocoa Church of God State Office and as a Commissioner and Chairman of the Housing Authority Board of Daytona Beach appointed by the Mayor of Daytona Beach in 2018. He is a 1985 graduate of Lee University in Cleveland, Tennessee with a Bachelor of Biblical Studies with an emphasis on Pastoral Ministry. He has worked toward a Master of Divinity at Pittsburgh Theological Seminary in Pittsburgh, Pennsylvania and the Pentecostal Theological Center in Cleveland, Tennessee.

He has served as a Pastor in Providence, Rhode Island, Baltimore, Maryland and on the island of Bermuda. His Evangelistic ministry has reached throughout the -United Sates, Canada, the West Indies, Europe, South Africa, Singapore, India, The United Emirates as well as Australia. He has also been a guest several times on Daystar television and a Keynote Speaker at the General Assembly of the Church of God in 1998 held in the Alamo Done in San Antonio, Texas and in that same year he founded "Lee Ministries International

Incorporated". In 2022, Rev Lee was elected as Chairman of the Church of God Executive Council of 18 a first for a person of color.

He serves as a mentor and a teacher for many young ministers in the Kingdom of God. He is married to the former Sheila Renee Freeland of Washington, D.C. and together they are sold out to a life of servant hood. It is the vision of this ministry to continue to evangelize the world for the Lord Jesus Christ and to prepare the next generation to be effective and powerful citizens in the Kingdom.

BIBLIOGRAPHY

Edwards, Gene "A Tale of Three Kings" Tyndale House Publishers Inc Carol Stream, Illinois. copyright 1980.

Swindoll, Charles "David- A Man of Passion and Destiny" Word Publishing, Dallas, Texas copyright 1997.

Ryken, Leland. "Dictionary of Biblical Imagery" Inter Varsity Press. Downers Grove, Illinois. Copyright 1998

Comay, Joan. "Who's who in the Bible" Wings Books. New York 1980

Websters New World Dictionary Third College Edition Copyright 1988

Spiros, Zodhiates. "The Complete Word Study Dictionary" AMG publishers Chattanooga, Tennessee 1992

Vine, W.E. Vine Expository Dictionary of Old and New Testament Thomas Nelson Publishers 1985

Lockyer, Herbert. "All The Kings and Queens of the Bible" Zondervan Publishing House. Grand Rapids, Michigan 1961

Narramore, Clyde "The Psychology of Counseling" Zondervan publishing Grand Rapids, Michigan 1960

Printed in Great Britain
by Amazon

46487877R00089